A User-Friendly Dictionary of Old English and Reader

Fifth Edition

Compiled by Bill Griffiths

Heart of Albion

A User-Friendly Dictionary of Old English and Reader

Fifth Edition

Compiled by Bill Griffiths

ISBN 1 872883 85 0

First published by author 1989
Third edition published by Heart of Albion Press 1993
Fifth edition (with reader) 2005

© Copyright Bill Griffiths 1989, 2005

The moral rights of the author have been asserted.
All rights reserved. No part of this book may be reproduced
in any form or by any means without prior written
permission from Heart of Albion Press, except for
brief passages quoted in reviews.

Heart of Albion

2 Cross Hill Close, Wymeswold
Loughborough, L|E12 6UJ

albion@indigogroup.co.uk

Visit our Web site: www.hoap.co.uk

Contents

Abbreviations	iv
Old English pronunciation	v
Inflections	vi
Introduction	1
nouns	2
gender	5
strong and weak nouns	7
adjectives	7
pronouns	8
this and that	10
verbs	12
present participle	13
the past tense	14
the past or passive participle	15
the imperative	15
the subjunctive	16
the infinitive	16
auxiliary verbs	17
adverbs	17
prepositions	17
conjunctions	19
word order	21
Reader of Old English	22
the everyday	22
history	31
heroic literature	35
laws and charters	39
the church	43
saints' lives	45
science	49
medicine	52
Dictionary	55

ABBREVIATIONS

acc.	accusative case (object)
adj.	adjective
adv.	adverb
comp.	comparative
conj.	conjunction
dat.	dative case (indirect object, agent)
F.	strong feminine noun
f.	weak feminine noun
gen.	genitive case (possessive)
I	class 1 weak verbs
II	class 2 weak verbs
indecl.	indeclinable
instr.	instrumental case (agent)
M.	strong masculine noun
m.	weak masculine noun
N.	strong neuter noun
n.	weak neuter noun
nom.	nominative (subject)
obl.	oblique cases i.e. those other than nominative
p.	preterite or past tense of verb
pl.	plural
pp.	past (or passive) participle of verb
ppl.	preterite (past) plural of verb
pref.	prefix
prep.	preposition
pron.	pronoun
sg.	singular
sim.	similarly
subj.	subjunctive of verb (wish, order)
subst.	substantive (noun)
superl.	superlative

OLD ENGLISH PRONUNCIATION

a (back 'a') short as in German M**a**nn   long as in f**a**ther

æ (front 'a') short as in c**a**t   long as in **a**dd

e short as in s**e**t long as in th**ey**

i short as in s**i**t   long as in mach**i**ne

o short as in g**o**t   long as in g**o**

u short as in s**oo**t   long as in h**oo**t

y was pronounced like French 'u' ('oo' with rounded lips) or German 'ü'; but in late West Saxon texts, 'y' becomes largely equivalent to 'i' and doubtless was pronounced like 'i'.

Note: unlike Modern English, the short and long forms of each vowel differ only as regards length; the sound of the vowel itself does not alter.

All consonants are sounded: e.g. *cniht* = c+n+i+h+t

The following special combinations should be noted:

    sc is pronounced sh

    cc is pronounced ch

    cg is pronounced dg

    ht is pronounced like kt (better, as in German ni**ch**t)

Note: g and c, in combination with back vowels (a, o, u) are pronounced as in go and kite. In combination with front vowels (æ, e, i) g and c are pronounced as in yacht and cheese: these latter (palatalised) forms are marked in the Dictionary with a dot, so that

    ġ = y   ċ = ch.

Such markings are necessarily tentative; for example, I regard ng as a single sound, not liable to palatalisation, and so give cyninge not cyninġe.

Note: there are two forms of the special OE consonant for th:

    þ, ('thorn') and ð ('eth') – in OE usage there are interchangeable.

INFLEXIONS

Unlike Modern English, which depends on the order of words in the sentence (sense-order) to convey meaning and fix the grammatical role of each word, OE had built-in word-endings or inflexions that served as markers for the role the word played in the sentence. Sense-order was thus less important in OE (especially in poetry). and eventually the student will have to come to grips with the four cases OE nouns exhibit:

nominative is used for the subject (the actor or doer) of a verb e.g. <u>he</u> ate cheese, the <u>king</u> liked cheese.

accusative is used for the direct object (the victim) of a verb e.g. he ate <u>cheese</u>.

the *genitive* is the possessive case: the <u>king's</u> cheese, the cheese <u>of Essex</u>.

the *dative* is used for the indirect object e.g. he gave cheese <u>to the mouse</u> as well as for the ablative or causative (agent) case e.g. the cheese was eaten <u>by the mouse</u>.

A case-ending in OE therefore often takes the place of words like 'of, 'to', 'by' etc. in Modern English.

Nouns in OE have gender (masculine, feminine, neuter) as in modem German. The principal case endings for 'strong' (meaning idiosyncratic or awkward!) nouns are as follows:

Strong Masculine Nouns (singular):	Strong Masculine Nouns (plural);
nom. — (no special ending)	*nom.* -as
acc. — (no special ending)	*acc.* -as
gen. -es	*gen.* -a
dat. -e	*dat.* -um

Neuter Nouns vary from the Masculine in having *nom./acc.pl.* without ending (compare Modern English plural 'sheep') or in -u rather than in -as.

Strong Feminine Nouns (singular):	Strong Feminine Nouns (plural):
nom. -u (or no ending)	*nom.* -a or -e
acc. -e	*acc.* -a or -e
gen. -re	*gen.* -ra
dat. -re	*dat.* -um

There is also a group of 'weak' nouns, which have all cases (other than *nom .sg.* and *dat.pl.*) in -an (cf. Modem English plural 'oxen').

Verbs take endings rather like those preserved in the Authorised King James Bible:

Present Tense: *ic bind-e* (I bind), *þu bindest* (you bind), *he bindeð* (he binds); the plural has just one ending: *bind-að* (we, you, they bind). The 3rd person sg. is often abbreviated in West Saxon to -t e.g. *he bin-t* besides Anglian *bind-eð*.

Past Tense: as in Modern English, there are two ways of making the past tense. With strong verbs the root vowel alters: *he biteð* (he bites) with *he bit* (he bit); *he swimmeð* (he swims) with *he swom* (he swam); with 'weak' verbs a suffix -ede (class I) or -ode (class II) is added e.g. *he ricsað* (he rules) with *he ricsode* (he ruled), *he lufað* (he loves) with *he lufode* (he loved). A variant is: *he ðenceð* (he thinks) with *he ðohte* (he thought). The past plural is always -on e.g. *lufodon*, etc.

The past participle is formed in -en for strong verbs, in -ed for weak verbs (much as in Modern English) e.g. *growen* (grown), *drifen* (driven), *ascod* (asked). The unstressed prefix ge- is usually added to the past participle e.g. *gedrifen, ge-ascod*); the same prefix can also impart a more emphatic, conclusive role to the verb e.g. ge-ascode 'learned by asking'.

The principal common suffixes or word-endings are as follows. Note, many of these were already ambiguous in OE, which probably contributed to their decline in use in the change-over into Modern English:

A	*gen.pl.* of all nouns, *nom.sg.* of weak nouns
A	*nom.acc.pl.* of Feminine nouns; *obl.sg.* of some nouns
ADE	ending for past of weak verbs (class II)
AN	infinitive of verb ('to do' etc.)
AN	ending of most cases in weak nouns and adjs.
AS	*nom.acc.pl.* ending of strong masculine nouns (compare Mod.E. plural in -s)
AÐ	third nerson sg. ending of present tense of weak verbs (class II)
E	*dat.sg.* of strong masculine and neuter nouns.

E		*nom./acc.pl.* of strong feminine nouns, and of all adjectives
E		common verb ending in present and past tense
EDE		ending for past tense of weak verbs (class I)
ES		*gen.* of strong masculine and neuter nouns (compare Mod.E. –'s)
EÐ		third person sg. ending of present tense of verbs (compare biblical 'seeketh' etc.)
IAÐ		plural ending of present tense of weak verbs (class II)
EDE		ending for past tense of weak verbs (compare Mod.E. –ed)
ON		plural ending of past tense of verbs
U		*nom.acc.pl.* of strong neuter noun; *nom.sg.* of some strong feminine nouns
UM		*dat.pl.* of all nouns; sometimes used to form an adverb from a noun
UM		*dat.sg.* of strong adj.

This dictionary also serves as a key to a range of further
Old English texts accessible online at
www.indigogroup.co.uk/oereader/

INTRODUCTION

Old English was the language spoken and written by the Anglo-Saxons in this island, between their arrival in the 5th century A.D. and the 12th century, by when the language was already modifying in reaction to the influence of Vikings in the North and the domination by Normans after the decisive Battle of Hastings in 1066.

At first sight OE (Old English) looks dauntingly alien. Then you begin to detect glimmers of similarity with Modern English – words like *ond* (and), þu (thou) and *leornung* (learning). Sometimes the similarities are misleading: OE *drēam* means not 'dream', but 'joy' or 'exultation'; OE *sellan* means 'to give' not 'to sell'. And the pronunciation of vowels is disturbingly different (less so if you live in the North of England). The language has changed so much in terms of vocabulary, pronunciation and grammar, that it is hard to believe sometimes that OE is the true ancestor of Modern English. Yet, despite the difficulties, the effort of learning something of OE is thoroughly rewarding: not only does it reveal the bone structure (as it were) of today's English, but its literature is unequalled in Europe at that time, and still justly admired as a great cultural resource, if difficult of access. Translations never do OE poetry justice. Much better to work a little and enjoy the reward of reading the original, whatever the barriers a thousand years of language change have put in the way.

An initial problem is the slightly different set of letters. þ (called 'thorn') and ð (called 'eth') both represent /th/. æ (called 'ash') is an /a/ rather from the front of the mouth (the /a/ in 'cat' or the Northern /a/ in 'Newcastle'). So far so good, but the spelling can be confusingly free. /i/ and /y/ become interchangeable in late OE texts, for example. Be prepared to be imaginative in recognising words in different guises!

The complexity of OE grammar is the serious problem. Old English is an inflected language with a variety of case endings, not unlike modern German. That is, the endings or suffixes of nouns and verbs vary according to their role in the sentence. There are traces of this in Modern English: verbs can have an /s/ added in the present (he sees, she writes, etc.), or an /ed/ in the past (he spotted, etc.). Nouns take an /s/ in the plural (many hills, etc.) and also for the possessive or genitive case (the king's crown, the woman's hand, etc.). Nonetheless, the role of inflexions in Modern English has been drastically simplified.

Full inflectional charts of Old English are rather daunting. Some principal ones (the ones you need to know) will be included here, but there is little point trying to learn them all off by heart at one go. Familiarise yourself with them, then try reading a little text, then learn some of the common vocabulary, and so, by turns, gradually work your way up.

Nouns

Nouns are words that represent things, commodities, ideas... (a stone, a table, wood, behaviour, writing, etc.)

In OE, as in Modern English, there are only two 'numbers' or levels of counting: singular and plural. (cyning 'the king', cyningas 'kings'). Another example:

 Twēġen heortas & ǣnne bār (two harts and one boar)

Both singular and plural have four cases or potential grammatical roles represented by different case endings, and this often stumps people used to Modern English, where endings like this have largely disappeared. But it is necessary to grasp the nettle and learn how the four cases work.

The **nominative** (nom.) or naming case is used for the subject of a sentence: the subject is the one who acts or does, so the combination is usually subject + verb:

 Iċ gā ūt on dæġrǣd (I go out at daybreak) – the subject is 'I'

 Hunta iċ ēom. (hunter I am i.e. I am a hunter) – note: the verb 'to be' can have two equal subjects: 'hunter' and 'I'

 Ēodon þā wyrmas (went then the dragons i.e. the dragons went away) – 'dragons' are the subject

The nominative case is often contrasted with the **accusative** (acc.) or object case. This represents the direct object or 'target' of an action:

 Iċ bidde ðē (I command you) – 'I' is the subject (nom.), 'you' the object (acc.)

 Hē tōdǣlde dæġ wið nihte (he divided day from night) – 'he' is the subject (nom.) 'day' is the object (acc.)

 Wulfwī mē wrāt (Wulfwiġ me wrote i.e. Wulfwiġ wrote me) – 'Wulfwiġ' is the subject (nom.), 'me' the object (acc.)

> Iċ sceal erian fulne æcer (I must plow a full field) 'I' is the subject (nom.), 'field' the object (acc.)
>
> Hwīlon sylþ mē hors (sometimes he-gives me a horse) – here the subject 'he' is unexpressed in the OE – the verb on its own stands for 'he gives'; 'horse' is the object (acc.)

The difference between subject and object is important – 'the king fears the peasant' is very different in its implications from 'the peasant fears the king'. But awkwardly there is often no special ending for the accusative (object) case of a noun. Pronouns are more obvious: *Iċ* ('I') can only be the subject: it becomes *mē* when it is the object. There are other ways of marking the object (note *fulne æcer;* above, where the *–ne* ending is an accusative inflexion for the adjective). In general, the order will be subject-verb-object as in Modern English, but as in examples above there is slightly more flexibility in this respect in OE than in Modern English.

The accusative has another use besides representing the object of a sentence: it can also be used to express a length of time:

> Hē hæfde þæt rīċe .xvi. ġēar (He had i.e. held or ruled the kingdom (for) 16 years) – where *ġēar* (years) is an uninflected neuter plural – in the acc. case nonetheless!

The **genitive** or possessive case is simpler to recognise. In Modern English it is expressed either by apostrophe-/s/ (the king's dog, etc) or by the use of 'of' (the dog of the king, etc.). In OE only the first of these two options is available: *cyninges hund* (the king's dog). Some examples are:

> Godes englas (God's angels)
>
> Grendeles pyt (Grendel's pit)
>
> Sceapes smerwe (sheep's grease)
>
> Westsēaxna cyning (the West Saxons' king, or king of the West-Saxons)

but:

> Nihta ġenipu (the nights' darknesses, or the shades of the nights) – the ending in /a/ is different because it is the genitive of plural noun.

The genitive also has more than one role: it can indicate the 'object' of certain verbs and then has the meaning 'in respect of':

> Ǣses brūcan (of-food to-enjoy i.e. the enjoy food)

> & his ġefæġene wǣrun (and of-him glad they-were i.e. and they rejoiced to see him)
>
> Ġeunn ūs tō þissum dæġe dæġhwāmlīċes fōstres. (Grant us for this day (our) daily food. – genitive endings in /es/)

And can be used of a point in time:

> and ðæs seofoþan dæġes hē ġereste hine
>
> (and on-the seventh day he rested himself.)

The fourth and last case is called the **dative** (or giving) case. It represents the indirect object, the person to whom something is given rather the thing actually given. In Modern English this is usually represented by using 'to' e.g. 'he gives the book to me' (where 'me' is the indirect object). Old English does not need the extra word 'to' – the dative (dat.) ending tells us that a word is the indirect object:

> Hwæt sylþ hē þē? (what gives he to-you?)
>
> Iċ sylle cynge swā-hwæt-swā iċ ġefō (I give to-the-king whatever I capture) – note the extra –/e/, the dative ending, on the noun *cyng*)
>
> Þā salde se here him foreġīslas (then gave the (Viking) army to-him hostages i.e. then the Vikings gave him hostages)
>
> Syllan beorhte blēda beornum and ðearfum (to give bright crops to (rich) men and needy) – the –/um/ ending is one of the most easy to recognise in OE – it always represents the dative plural, though sometimes the dative plural is used as an adverb e.g. *hwīlum* (at times, sometimes), *miċlum* (greatly).

Another common use of the dative case is to represent the 'agent', the person or thing by which something is done. Paradoxically he, she or it is really the subject of the action, but this is turned round in a passive verb:

> Wætre beworpen (by-water surrounded)
> Flōr forste ġeworuht. (floor by/of-frost made)
> Wealle beworhton (by-(a)-wall built-round i.e. surrounded)
>
> Brim sceal sealte weallan (the-sea must with-salt seethe)

The dative has several other uses in OE, which can usually be translated by prefixing the word 'to'…

> Lēaf & gærs…blōweð & grōweð eldum tō āre (leaf and grass…blossoms and grows to-men as (a) benefit i.e. for the benefit of men)

Sibb is ēġhwǣm lēofost (concord is to-everyone dearest)

Eorla ġehwām ēadnys and tōhīht (and (to) mens' each (a) blessing and (a) hope) – literally 'of men to each' where ġehwǣm ('to each') is the dative and eorla ('of men') is a genitive plural. This type of phrase is common in OE poetry.

Hors hōfum wlanc ((a) horse in-respect-of-its-hoofs glorious i.e. a horse, glorious in its hoofs)

Ġimmum ġelīcust (to-gems most-like i.e. most resembling gems)

The dative is also used to follow some prepositions:

gold on grēote (gold on the-ground)

tō þǣre ēċan reste (to that eternal rest)

and with certain verbs:

God helpe mīnum handum (God help i.e. guide my hands)

Swā him bebēad Meotud (as to-him bade God i.e. as God ordered him)

Ġewīton him þā Norðmenn (departed – the Northmen) note: here the *him* is redundant in Modern English, it is quasi-reflexive: 'took themselves away'

Gender

Another attribute of nouns is gender. We may be familiar (and mildly amused) by nouns having a gender in foreign languages like French and German, but in Anglo-Saxon times, this was also the situation in English. The three genders are of course: masculine, feminine and neuter (he, she, it). In modern English, 'it' can only refer to things. In OE, its implication is the child or pre-adult rather than the inanimate thing – *ċild* (child) and *mæġden* (maiden) are both neuter nouns; but *it* is also used for impersonal verbs, much as in Modern English ('it is cold', 'it snows', etc.)

The three genders are not just the invention of grammarians (busy already in Roman and Anglo-Saxon times). That men's names in OE end in masculines nouns (e.g. Wulf-stān), and women's names end in feminine nouns (e.g. Ælf-ġyfu) shows that a basic sense of the gender of nouns applied. But in most cases, the gender of a noun is a grammatical fact, having little to do with its 'natural' gender e.g. *ġēar* ('year' – neuter), *frēondscipe* ('friendship' – feminine), and, rather startling, *þæt wīf* (the woman, neuter). Nouns that we regard as neuter ('it') are more usually masculine or feminine in OE – a point that some find hard to get their heads round.

The importance of gender is that it defines different types of nouns that have different sets of endings for the cases. So far, we have generally dealt with the commonest type of masculine noun:

Nom.sg.	cyning	(nominative singular – subject – the king)
Acc.sg.	cyning	(accusative singular – object – the king)
Gen.sg.	cyninges	(genitive singular – possessive – the king's, of the king)
Dat.sg.	cyninge	(dative singular – indirect object – to the king)
Nom.pl.	cyningas	(nominative plural – subject – the kings)
Acc.pl.	cyningas	(accusative plural – object – the kings)
Gen.pl.	cyninga	(genitive plural – possessive – the kings', of the kings)
Dat.pl.	cyningum	(dative plural – indirect object – to the kings)

But there is an alternative set of endings for a comparable feminine noun:

Nom.sg.	ġiefu	(nominative singular – subject – a gift)
Acc.sg.	ġiefe	(accusative singular – object – a gift)
Gen.sg.	ġiefe	(genitive singular – possessive – of the gift)
Dat.sg.	ġiefe	(dative singular – indirect object – to or by the gift)
Nom.pl.	ġiefa	(nominative plural – subject – gifts)
Acc.pl.	ġiefa	(accusative plural – object – gifts)
Gen.pl.	ġiefa	(genitive plural – possessive – of the gifts)
Dat.pl.	ġiefum	(dative plural – indirect object – to or by the gifts)

The neuter noun follows the endings of the masculine, except that its nom/acc plural is either endingless (usually with words of one syllable in the nom.sg.) or in –/u/ (for words of several syllables).

Strong and Weak Nouns

The inflexions for the noun that we have met so far are called 'strong' endings (strong is the sense of dominant, idiosyncratic, awkward). A further set are called 'weak' endings (more regular, compliant, predictable). Fortunately, they are quite simple to learn, as most cases end in –/an/.

Nom.sg.	steorra	(nominative/subject – the star)
Acc.sg.	steorran	(accusative/object – the star)
Gen.sg.	steorran	(genitive/possessive – the star's)
Dat.sg.	steooran	(dative/indirect object – to the star)
Nom.pl	steorran	(the stars)
Acc.pl.	steorran	(the stars)
Gen.pl.	steorrena	(of the stars)
Dat.pl	steorrum	(to the stars)

Adjectives

Adjectives are words that describe or amplify a noun: the *blue* sky, *many* times, a *sharp* sword, etc. Many OE adjectives are easily recogniable: *rēad* (red), *cwiċ* (alive, quick), *hefiġ* (heavy) etc.

Adjectives are also inflected, in accordance with the noun they describe. More, the adjective has both a set of strong and weak endings, and any adjective can take either set of endings. Which set of endings is applies depends on the way the adjective is used.

If the adjective stands alone before the noun, without a preceding 'article', strong endings are used (regardless of whether the noun is strong or weak!):

    Mid sweartum gāstum (with dark ghosts) – dat.pl.

    Ordfruma ælcre sprǣċe (the-origin of-all speech) – gen.sg. (feminine noun)

    Miċle āþas (great oaths) – nom/acc.pl.

(The endings are similar to those of the strong noun, but note nom/acc.pl. in –/e/ not -/as/)

If the adjective is used with a definite article or the like in front, the weak set of endings is used:

> Þā rēadan blōmas (the red flowers) – nom.pl.
>
> Se feaxeda steorra (the hairy star i.e. comet) – nom.sg.
>
> Þes foresǣda hālga wer (this aforementioned holy man) – nom.sg.

Because the ending is often different in the adjective and the noun it 'agrees' with, the ending an adjective shows can be a useful indicator of case (however awkward to learn).

Some other facts about adjectives:

An adjective can be used as a noun (as a substantive). In that case the definite article is followed by the weak adjectival endings:

> þā yflan (the evil ones) etc.

The comparative and superlative forms of adjectives are similar to those in Modern English:

> Rēad, rēadra, rēadost (red, redder, reddest) – note the comparative form – *rēadra* – is always given weak adjective endings
>
> Sum, māra, mǣst (some, more, most)
>
> Manna mildust ond monðwǣrust, / lēodum līðost ond lōfġeornost (of men the gentlest and most-sympathetic, to-his-people the kindest and most-keen-of-approval – said of Beowulf)

Pronouns

A pronoun is a word that stands in place of a noun. The obvious examples are the 'personal' pronouns: I, you, he, she, it, they. A pronoun is interchangeable with a noun, thus *se cyning rīt* (the king rides) can equally be expressed as *he rīt* (he rides). But words like 'who', 'which', 'that' can also serve as pronouns.

First the personal pronoun:

First Person:

Nom.sg.	Iċ	(I)	Nom.pl.	wē	(we)
Acc. sg.	mē	(me)	Acc.pl.	ūs	(us)
Gen.sg.	mīn	(mine)	Gen.pl	ūre	(our)
Dat.sg.	mē	(to me)	Dat.pl.	ūs	(to us)

(note the genitive forms are in fact adjectives, 'my', 'our')

Second Person:

Nom.sg.	ðu	(you)	Nom.pl.	gē	(ye)
Acc.sg.	ðē	(thee)	Acc.pl.	gē	(ye)
Gen.sg.	ðīn	(thine)	Gen.pl.	ēower	(your)
Dat.sg.	ðē	(to thee)	Dat.pl.	ēow	(to ye)

Third Person:

Nom.sg.	hē (he)	hēo (she)	hit (it)
Acc.sg.	hine (him)	hī (her)	hit (it)
Gen.sg.	his (his)	hīre (her)	his (its)
Dat.sg.	him (to him)	hīre (to her)	him (to it)

(whether you translate any particular example as 'he', 'she' or 'it' depends in Modern English on whether it is a person or a thing. In OE the form will depend on the gender of the noun referred to!)

The plural of the third person is the same for all genders, though disturbingly unlike the Modern English:

Nom.pl.	hī	(they)
Acc.pl.	hī	(them)
Gen.pl	heora	(their)
Dat.pl	him	(to them)

Remarks:

OE *hit* (it) can be used impersonally with verbs, as in Modern English:

> Hit snīweð (it snows)
>
> Hit is... (it is...)
>
> Miċel ġedeorf ys hyt (great toil is it)

And as the 'object' in a reflexive verb:

> Hēr hīene bestǣl se here on midne winter ofer tuelftan niht to Ċippanhamme (Here itself bestole the army on middle winter at Twelfth Night to Chippenham i.e. the (Viking) army 'took itself')

'Who', 'what' – the interrogative pronouns (used in asking questions) are different again:

Nom.sg.	hwā...
Acc.sg.	hwone
Gen.sg.	hwæs
Dat.sg.	hwǣm, hwām

Note the neuter nom/acc *hwæt* (Modern English 'what') and an instrumental form *hwy* (by what?).

As interrogative pronouns, these are used much as in Modern English e.g. 'Hwæt sæġest þu?' (what say you?) – but are only used in asking questions, not as relative pronouns in Modern English. We can say 'the woman who has a gold ring' but the OE equivalent will be found in the next section.

This and That

OE has two words, *þes* and *þæt*, rather as in Modern English. You can call them demonstrative adjectives, but *þæt* often stands on its own, without implying any contrast to 'this'. Unlike Modern English, an article is not necessary before a noun: *cyning* translates as 'king' or 'the king' or 'a king'. OE *þæt* always has a slightly stronger force than simply 'the', and can translate 'the' or 'that/those' according to context.

Þæt is in fact the neuter form – there are masculine and feminine (used according to the gender of the following noun), singular and plural, for all four cases! All of these are very common in OE, so are given here in full and are worth learning. In fact, they are not wildly new endings – they resemble the personal pronouns (and the strong nouns):

Nom.sg.	se (M.)	sēo (F.)	þæt (N.)
Acc.sg	þone	þā	þæt
Gen.sg.	þæs	þǣre	ðæs
Dat.sg.	þǣm	þǣre	þǣm
Nom.pl.	þā		
Acc.pl.	þā		
Gen.pl.	þāra		
Dat.pl.	þǣm		

There are no masculine, feminine and neuter forms of the word 'the' in Modern English – we use the one word for every gender and every case. In OE which gender and case are used depends on the noun the demonstrative is used with: if the noun is nom.masc.sg then <u>se</u> will be used, if dat.pl then *þǣm*, etc.:

> se cyning (since the noun is masculine; <u>se</u> indicates it must be nom.sg.)
>
> þǣm cyning (to the king) – dat.sg.
>
> þǣm cyningum (to the kings) – here the ending of the noun shows it is dat.pl.
>
> sēo cwene (the woman, queen) – fem.nom.sg
>
> þǣre cwene (of the woman), etc.

Interestingly, one of the commonest forms, *þā* in the plural, seems to be the origin of the Modern English word 'the' – the other cases and their endings have long been lost!

A rare extra form of se/sēo/þæt is the instrumental case which has one form: *þÿ, þē* (by that, by which):

> Hē scryt mē wel & fētt & hwīlon sylþ mē hors oþþe bēah, þæt **þē** lustlīcor cræft mīnne iċ begancge. (He clothes me well and feeds (me) and sometimes gives me (a) horse or (precious) ring, so-that by-that the-more-keenly my skill I exercise.)

> Þȳ ġēare þe wæs agān fram cristes aċennesse .cccc. wintra & xciiii wintra… (In-the year which was past from Christ's birth 400 winters i.e. years and 93 winters…)

The forms of se/sēo/þæt are also used as relative pronouns: 'the man whom I met' would be *se monn þone ic mette*; 'the woman to whom I gave a ring' would be *sēo cwene þǣre ic selde bēag*, etc.

Also, *þæt* or *þe* can be used in the above position, for any case, much as in Modern English:

> ðū **þe** færst on þone weġ (you that or who travels on the way)
>
> ġeong hæleð, **þæt** wæs god ælmihtiġ ((the) young hero, who was God almighty)
>
> Ūre fæder **þe** on heofonum eart (Our Father, who art in heaven…) – but note, the OE for 'heaven' is used in the plural – we also speak of 'the heavens'
>
> se dǣl, **se** þǣr niehst wæs (the part, that thereto nearest was)

OE *þes* is less commonly used than OE *þæt*, but is also worth setting out:

Nom.sg.	þes (M.)	þēos (F.)	þis (N.)
Acc.sg	þisne	þās	þis
Gen.sg.	þisses	þisse	þisses
Dat.sg.	þissum	þisse	þissum
Nom.pl.	þās		
Acc.pl.	þās		
Gen.pl.	þissa		
Dat.pl.	þīssum		

Plus an instrumental form: *þȳs*

Verbs

A verb represents action, it is like the engine giving motion to the train-sentence. In Modern English it can be a single word (e.g. 'runs', 'hurts') or a group of words (a phrasal verb – 'am sitting', 'will be coming', etc.). In OE, the verb is essentially a single word, and can be used without a subject being expressed. Thus *is* can mean 'is', 'he is', 'she is', 'it is'. Examples:

Dēst (you do, you are doing)

Cumað (they come, they are coming)

Eteð (eats, he eats, he is eating, she eats, etc.)

As OE only has two tenses: present and past, the present sometimes also has to stand for the future: thus *bið* can mean both 'is' and 'will be', according to context.

The endings of the present tense are like those you may be familiar with from the King James Bible (e.g. 'he saith', 'she hath', 'he casteth'):

Iċ gange (I go)

Ðu gangest (thou goest)

Hē gangeð (he goeth)

Wē gangað (we go)

Ġē gangað (you go, plural)

Hī gangað (they go)

In some verbs, expecially in West Saxon, the forms for the 2nd and 3rd persons sg (thou, he) contract, with change of the stem vowel:

Hē cymð than he cumeð (comes)

Sēo hæfð than sēo hafað (has) etc.

Verbs with the infinitive in –ian e.g. *lufian* (to love) have slightly different present tense forms:

Iċ lufie

Ðū lufast

He lufað

Wē, Ġē, Hī lufiað

Present Participle

This is not used as in Modern English to form the continuous present of a verb ('we are working', etc.), but more as an adjective, or as the verbal element in a dependant clause:

þywende oxon to felda (driving (the) oxen to (the) field)

iċ þǣr tōġeanes standende (I there opposite standing)

The Past Tense

The past tense is also called the preterite. The endings are fairly regular, but it is important to note two classes of verbs, strong and weak (awkward and conformable). The weak verbs have the simplest past forms in –/ed/ (often contracted to /d/):

> Hæfde (he/she/it had)
>
> Lifdon (they lived)

Verbs with the infinitive in –ian form the past with -/od/:

> Lufian – he lufode (loved)
>
> Macian – he macode (made)

Sometimes these are shortened to give –t:

> Hē brōhte (brought), sōhte (sought), þōhte (thought) – much as in Modern English, in fact.

The past of a strong verb is less regular, as it usually involves a change in the stem vowel:

> Hē swimeð (he swims) – hē swam (he swam)
>
> Hē farað (he travels) – hē fōr (he went)
>
> Hī cumað (they come) – hī cōmon (they came)
>
> Đu rītst (you ride) – ðu ride, he rād (rode)

Again, is quite like the way some Modern English verbs behave in the past tense – swim/swam, come/came, see/saw etc. There are some seven different classes of strong verbs in OE, but rather than spend time on them now, it will be enough to have a basic idea of how strong and weak verbs behave, and learn the forms of individual verbs as you read texts.

However, some some irregular verbs do need to be listed:

Bēon – to be   Dōn – to do

Iċ ēom, bēo   Iċ dō

Đū eart / bist   ðū dēst

Hē is / bið   hē dēð

Wē sint / sindon/ earon   wē dōþ

With past:

Hē wæs, hī wæron.   Hē dyde, hī dydon

The Past or Passive Participle

In Modern English this is used both in forming the 'perfect' (or complete) tenses (they have *seen*, she had *swum*, I had *arrived*) and in the passive (I was being *watched*, he was *killed*, she is *loved*, etc.). The 'passive' voice of the verb is one in which the subject of the verb is also the object (the doer as well as the recipient of the action).

To form the passive voice, the verb *beon* (to be) or *weorðan* (to become) is followed by the passive (past) participle:

> Iċ ēom lufod (I am loved)
>
> ān wulf wearð āsend (a wolf was sent)

Note that the past participle of weak verbs is formed in –/ed/, -/od/, that of strong verbs in –/en/ – a distinction retained in Modern English. Examples of strong verbs:

> Ġedrefen (driven), ġesungen (sung), ġesēon (seen), etc.

(Note that this participle usually takes the unaccented prefix /ġe-/ (pronounced /yeh/) – in Middle English this reduces to /i-/I or /y-/ before disappearing completely in Modern English.)

The Imperative

The imperative of the verb is the form used to give an order. As this can look the same as other parts of the verb in Modern English, we use an exclamation mark to make its role clear: 'go!', 'stop!' 'don't...!' etc.

In OE, the imperative is either the stem of the verb or ends in -/e/, -/a/:

> **Dō** þās wyrta on ān fæt, **sete** under wēofod, **sing** ofer IX mæssan (put these herbs in a vessel, set (it) under (the) altar, sing over (it) nine masses)
>
> Ūs ġemildsa (forgive or be be merciful (to) us)
>
> Ā **sy** ðīn nama ēċelīċe ġebletsod (ever be thy name eternally blessed)

The Subjunctive

A different mode of verb, seldom if ever encountered in Modern English, is known as the subjunctive (literally, subordinate or alternative). In this mode, the verb expresses not just action but the need for action, almost an order. A possible example in Modern English is 'save' in 'God save the queen' – subtly different from 'God saves the queen' or 'God, save the queen!'. The ending, -/e/ can overlap with the imperative form, but the plural in -/en/ is distinctive:

> Ġeselle him mon .lx. scillinga (give to-him (the) man 60 shillings i.e. the guilty man shall pay the victim 60 shillings)
>
> Þe Deuel þē **habbe** (the Devil thee have i.e. may the Devil take you)

A common use of the subjunctive in OE is in subordinate clauses, where it usually implies uncertainty, possibility, indefiniteness:

> þy lǣs iċ **drunce** & þone mīnne þeġn **þyrste** (in case I should-drink and him, my soldier, make-thirst)

The Infinitive

The infinitive (unfinished or unclosed) form of the verb – as opposed the finite or active/complete forms – is represented in Modern English as 'to be', 'to run', 'to sing' etc. In OE it is a single word, and takes the ending –/an/. It is the way verbs are usually quoted in OE dictionaries e.g. *singan* 'to sing', *bēon* 'to be' etc.

The infinitive is used with a finite verb to construct various compound or modal verbs (see below, under Auxiliary Verbs).

It can also have a passive sense as in:

> forlēron eorla ġestrēon eorðan healdan (they-abandoned men's treasure for-the-earth-to-hold, or by-the-earth to-be-held)

In the form *to singanne, to findanne,* etc. it represents not our modern 'to sing', 'to find', but has a sense of necessity: *to singanne* 'to be sung', *to findanne* 'to be found', etc. For example:

> bebēad tō healdanne (he ordered (the laws) to be observed)

Auxiliary Verbs

Auxiliary (assistant) verbs are used to form various modal or compound verbs in OE. In Modern English, examples are 'we may arrive', 'we ought to be', 'you can do it'. In OE, the second element is the infinitive of the verb, and a number of different auxiliary verbs can be used before the infinitve:

> With sense 'to will' or 'wish': wē willað gān (we want to-go – a little stronger than the Modern English 'we will go')
>
> – may: iċ mæġ gān (I may go), hī meahton gān (they might or could go)
>
> – shall, has to, must: hīo sceal gān (she must go)
>
> – can, knows how to: wē cunnon singan (we know how to sing)

Examples:

> Mid þysum fīf stafum man mæġ wrītan (with these five vowels one can write)
>
> Fisc sceal on wætere (the fish must in water – here the infinitive is omitted, the sense is almost 'the fish must live or belongs in water')

Adverbs

Adverbs are words that describe or modify a verb; go *quickly*, do that *more quietly*, he swims *regularly*, they *never* agree.

As a common ending for an adjective in OE is *–lic*, so a common form for an adverb is *–līċe* e.g. *frēondlīċe* (in a friendly way).

Adverbs can also be formed from the dative plural of a noun e.g. *willum* (gladly).

Prepositions

Prepositions are words that go before a noun, like 'to', 'from', 'by' etc. Modern English depends on these where OE would often use case endings e.g. 'of someone' takes the place of the OE genitive (possessive), 'to someone' or 'by someone' takes the place of the OE dative.

But a range of prepositions are important in their own right in OE, and are followed by nouns in an oblique case (not the nominative) – usually the acc. or the dat.

Æfter (along, through) – æfter wudum fōr (through the woods travelled)

Ǣr (before) – ǣr underne (before morning)

Æt (at, near) – lūtian æt hām (skulk at home)

Be (about) – hwæt dēst þū be þīnre huntunge? (What do you regards your hunting?)

Būton (without) – būtan nettum huntian iċ mæġ (without nets hunt I can)

Fram (from) – alȳs ūs fram yfele (deliver us from evil)

In (in or on) – biþ on telgum wlitiġ (it-is in (its) branches beautiful), wexeð on wature (flourishes in water)

(note: in/on are two forms of the same word in OE, either can be translated 'in' or 'on' in Modern English according to context; *in* is more usual in Northern texts)

Mid (with) – mid heora flȳse his fēt drygdon (with their fur his feet they-dried)

Of (from) – of heovenan into paradisum (out of the sky into Paradise)

Ofer (over, above) – *ofer dēop waeter* (over deep water)

Onmiddan (amidst) – onmiddan ðǣre flōre (in-the-middle of-the floor)

Under (below, near) – þæt hē bēo eall under eorðan (so that it be all underground)

Wið (against) – Wið þissum wyrmum wē fuhton (against these dragons we fought)

Ymb/e (around, after) – ymb ealra landa ġehwylċ (around all lands' each); ymbe fela wintra (after many winters i.e. years)

The preposition can sometimes be found following the noun – in that case it is technically a postposition:

& him tō cōmon þǣr onġēn Sumorsǣte alle (and him to i.e. to him, came there towards men-of-Somerset all)

Prepositions also commonly combine with verbs, but loosely, to form 'separable verbs':

beran ūt (to carry out)

ūtādrīfan, drīfeð ūt (drive out, expel)

Some verb prefixes like /a/- and /be/- have little effect on the meaning, though they can emphasise the transitive status of the verb (expecting an object); in a few cases they make a particular addition to the meaning e.g. the pronoun *to-* as a verb prefix expresses a scattering action: ex. *tōdǣlan* (to make disperse); while *for-* conveys a destructive sense e.g. *forbærne* (to destroy by burning); *oð-* has partitive force ex. *oðfeallan* (to fall away, decline), *oðscēotan* (to escape), *oðswerian* (to break an oath) and *of-* has an almost negative force: *ofgifan* (to give up), *ofhealdan* (to abandon).

A common prefix with verbs is /ġe/-, which denotes completeness or a further stage in the continuation of an action. It is almost always used to introduce the past/passive participle (e.g. ġebrungen 'brought', ġesēon 'seen'). But also it can form a new verb with modified meaning e.g. *acsian* 'to ask', *ġe-acsian* 'to learn by asking, to find out'.

Conjunctions

A clause, you will recall, is a part of a sentence with a finite verb. A sentence can comprise one clause or more than one clause, and in the second case it is usual to have a conjunction joining clause to clause.

A simple example would be:

I came *and* visited the town *but* the museum was shut.

This sort of structure is found quite often in the Anglo-Saxon Chronicle, where events in the same year are joined by a simple 'and' sign (in OE the sign is 7, but in extracts below we change this to **&** so make it more recognisable – it is pronounced *ond* or *and*).

Clauses joined by 'and' or 'but' are necessarily of equal importance. Other conjunctions introduce dependant or subordinate clauses, that help explain the main clause. Thus 'because', 'since', 'when', 'although' etc. in Modern English introduce a subordinate clause. The same syntax is used in OE. Some examples of conjunctions are:

Forðǣm/ðe (because) – ne sceal hunta forhtfull wesan, forþām mislīċe wildēor wuniað on wudum (not must (a) hunter timid be, because various wild-animals dwell in (the) woods)

Ġif (if) – ac hī mōston mid ealle þes cynges wille folgian ġif hī woldon libban oððe land habban (but they must entirely this king's will follow if they wished to-live or (their) land retain)

Oððe (or) – wrīt þūs oððe bet (write thus or better)

Oð (until) – oð hit cimeð to ðǣre diċ (until it comes to the ditch)

Siððan (since) – syððan up cume æðele sunne (once up comes (the) noble Sun) – also common as an adverb, 'then, next', afterwards'

Swā (as or when) – swa his fōt ġestōp (when his foot advanced)

Þā (when) – þā ðā hire tīma cōm (when her time came)

Þæs þe (after) – þæs þe hīe up cuōmon (after they up came i.e. landed)

Þonne (when; also 'than'): hwæþre hē swīðor mīnes fēores & ġesynto wilnade þonne his selfes (nonetheless he more-strongly for-my life and wellbeing wished than his (own))

Etc.

There are some peculiarities attaching to subordinate clauses in OE:

1. the verb of the subordinate clause may come at the end rather than in its expected position. Ex. þe þǣr lāfe wǣron (who there as-remnant were)

2. a subordinate clause can have a verb in the subjunctive – if so it tends to imply something unreal or potential about the action of the verb. (See above under The Subjunctive.)

3. some conjuctions, especially *þā* (when), can occur in pairs, in which case they are said to correlate, and the meaning is slightly different. The *þā* in the subordinate clause has the expected meaning 'when', the *þā* in the main clause (properly an adverb rather than a conjunction) translates as 'then' – though in Modern English we seldom need both:

þā hē ġefōr, þā feng his sunu Cynric tō þām rīċe (when he passed-on, then succeeded his son Cynric to the kingdom)

þā hē þā þæt wæter mē tō brōhte... þā hēt iċ mīn weorod & ealle mīne dugūþe tōsomne, & hit þā beforan heora ealra onsyne niðer āġēat

(when he that water me to brought... (then) ordered I my army and all my hearth-men together and it (then) before their all sight out poured)

Swā swīðe hē lufode þā hēadēor Swā swylċe hē wǣre heora fæder (So intensely he loved the tall deer as if he was their father)

Oððe on Offan Mercna cyninges oððe on Æþelbryhtes (either in
the laws of Offa, Mercians' king, or on Æþelbryht's)

Word order

Because nom. and acc. (subject and object) cases are not always distinguished in OE, the order of words tends to be the 'sense' order (subject – verb – object) as in Modern English. But equally, because OE is an inflected language, with word endings that indicate a word's role in the sentence, word order can vary, especially in poetry. Some variant sentence patterns are:

> Heortas iċ ġefengc on nettum (harts I catch in nets)
>
> & he lytle werede unīeþelice æfter wudum fōr (and he with-a-little troop in-difficulty through woods travelled)

After you have read some texts, you will come to appreciate the fluency and variety of prose that can be composed in OE. It takes a little while to gain a 'sense' of how OE works. Not only the grammar but the vocabulary has changed a lot. Unlike the grammar, which has become simpler, our modern vocabulary has become much more complex. This may not seem the case as you wrestle with strange words, but this only reflects the situation that a lot of OE words fell out of use by the start of the modern period. Their place was taken not only by French words and words from Old Norse, but by a rather intellectual range of words modelled on Latin and Greek. The subtlety of our vocabulary has continued expanding, so that a modern speaker will need to command (tens of) thousands of words. Be grateful, that in comparison, you only need to learn a few hundred words (some of them familiar anyway) to be able to cope with simple OE texts. We very much hope this booklet will help you in these early stages of reading OE.

Reader of Old English

1. The Everyday

Scribbles

These are the Anglo-Saxon equivalent of grafitti – small jottings in the margins of manuscripts, some serious, some playful. Not surprisingly, they often deal with the laborious process of writing the manuscript.

Ā scæl gelǣred smið swā hē ġelīcost mæġ be bīsne wyrcan būtan hē bet cunne

Ever must (a) skilled smith (go) as he most-like can from (this) sample do unless he better can. [For 'smith', understand 'scribe']

Iċ wǣt þæt ne ġeweorðað þæt Orm wēre swā wīs on bōcum swā hē is for werolde

I know that not it-will-be that Orm ?shall-be as wise in books as he is before (the) world(i.e. in worldly matters)

Be comēta þām steorran: ðȳllīċne lēoman hæfð comēta se steorra and on englics hine man nemð se feaxeda steorra. Hē hine ætȳwð seldan ymbe fela wintra and þonne for fortācne

About comet-the-star: this-like light has comet-the-star and in English it one names the well-haired star. It itself shows after many winters (i.e. years) and then as (a) warning/prediction.

God helpe mīnum handum

God help my hands i.e. guide them in writing

And iċ bidde ðē þæt þū mē wrīt þās VII vers and send mē.

And I ask you that you me write-out these 7 verses and send (them) to me

Ælfmǣr Patta-fox þū wilt swingan Ælfric ċild.

Ælfmær Patta-fox, you intend to-flog Æflric (the) child.

Wrīt þus oððe bet oððe þīne hȳde forlēt.

Write thus or better or your hide forfeit.

Mabbe þe Deuel þē habbe and bere tō his owene neste, and frete.

Mabbe-the-Devil you have and carry to his own nest, and devour.

On þisre worulde fruman God ælmihtig ġescēop and ġeworhte on syx dagum ealle ġesceafta, and ðæs seofoþan dæġes hē ġereste hine. And on syx ȳlda is þēos woruld ēac tōdǣled, and sēo seofoðe belimpð to þǣre ēcan reste.

On this world's beginningm God almighty shaped and wrought in six days all

Creatures/creation, and (on) the seventh day he rested himself. And on six ages ist his world also divided, and the seventh reblongs to the eternal rest.

Hēr hē ġesyndrode wæter and eorðan.

Here he parted water and earth.

Hēr hē tōdǣlde dæġ wið nihte.

Here he divided day from night (or light from darkness)

Hēr Godes englas āstīgan of heouenan intō paradisum.

Here God's angels ascend from (the) skies into paradise.

Hēr Drihten ġescōp Adames wīf Evam.

Here (the) Lord fashioned Adam's wife Eve.

Be sūðan wudigan ġæte æt Aclee on Westsǣxum on Laurentius mæssandaeġi on Wōdnesdæġi Ælfsiġe ðǣm biscope in his ġetelde Aldred se profast ðās fēower *collectæ* on fīf næht aldne mōna ǣr underne āwrāt.

By (the) southern gate at ?Oakleigh in Wessex on Laurence's mass-day on Wednesday (for) Ælfsige the bishop in his tent Aldred the provost these four 'collects' on (the) fifth night old moon before dawn wrote-out.

Sibb is ēġhwǣm lēofost

Concord is to-everyone dearest

Lyfinċ bisceop āh þās bōc.

Lyfinc (the) bishop owns this book

Wulfwī mē wrāt

Wulfwig me wrote

Cxnnb mbgf þx brædbn. Hwæt þks mbgf bfpn. Kc wfnf þæt hkt nks fðrædf.

(Cynna mage þȳ brǣdan hwæt þis mage bēon. Iċ wēne þæt hit nis eðrǣde.)

Sharp-wit can to-you make-clear what his can be. I believe that it is-not easy-to-read!

Ðis is *quinque uocales.* Mid þysum fīf stafum man mæġ wrītan, swā hwæt swā hē wile

This is (the) five vowels. With these five letters one can write whatever he wishes

Ðū þe fǣrst on þone weġ, grēt ðū mīnne brōðor, mīnre mōdor ċeorl.

You that travel on the way, greet you my brother, my mother's son.

From Ælfriċ's Colloquy:

Ælfriċ was one the most prolific and popular of Anglo-Saxon authors, especially noted for arranging saints' lives in a clear, attractive Old English style. He started out, however, as a teach of Latin in a monastery, and the following question-and-answer sequences were part of a handbook for learning Latin. An OE 'crib' (not by Ælfric) was later added, and this is sampled here. It is not particularly idiomatic OE as it reflects its Latin source, but is fascinating reading – especially they way the hard-done-by ploughman and tactiturn hunter are characterised.

The Ploughman

Hwæt sæġest þy, yrþlingc? Hū begæst þū weorc þīn?

What say you, ploughman? How perform you work yours?

Ēalā, lēof hlāford, þearle iċ deorfe.

O, dear master, hard I work.

Iċ gā ūt on dæġrǣd þywende oxon tō felda, & iugie hiġ tō sȳl.

I go out at dawn ('day-red') driving (the) oxen to (the) field, and yoke them to (the) plough.

Nys hit swā stearc winter þæt iċ durre lūtian æt hām for eġe hlāfordes mīnes, ac ġeiukodan oxan, & ġefæstnodon scēare mit þǣre sȳl, ælċe dæġ iċ sceal erian fulne æcer oþþe māre.

Not/never-is-it so harsh winter that I dare skulk at home for fear of-lord mine, but with-yoked ox and fixed share to the plough, each day I must plough (a) full acres (or field) or more.

Hæfst þū æniġne ġefēran?

Have you any companion/helper?

Iċ hæbbe sumne cnapan þywende oxan mid gādīsene, þe ēac swilċe nū hās ys for ċylde & hrēame.

I have a-certain youngster driving (the) ox with (a) goad, who al-so now hoarse is from (the) cold and shouting

Hwæt māre dēst þū on dæġ?

What more do you in (a) day?

Ġewyslīċe þænne māre iċ dō.

Surely then more I do

Iċ sceal fyllan binnan oxan mid hiġ, & wæterian hiġ, & scearn heora beran ūt.

I must fill (the) bins/mangers of-the-ox with hay, and water them, and muck their carry out.

Hiġ, Hiġ; miċel ġedeorf ys hyt.

O, O – (a) great toil is it!

Ġelēof, miċel ġedeorf hit ys, forþām iċ neom frēoh.

Dear-one, great toil it is, because I am-not free (i.e. am a slave)

The Hunter

Canst þū æniġ þing?

Do-know you any thing/skill?

Ǣnne cræft iċ cann.

One skill I know.

Hwylċne?

Which?

Hunta ic eom.

(A) hunter I am.

Hwæs?

Whose?

25

Cincges.

(The) king's.

Hū begæst þū cræft þīnne?

How practice you skill yours?

Iċ brēde mē max & sette hiġ on stōwe ġehæppre, & ġetihte hundas mīne þæt wildēor hiġ ēhton, oþþæt hiġ becuman tō þām nettan unforsceawodlīċe & þæt hiġ swā bēon begrynodo, & iċ ofslēa hiġ on þām maxum.

I knot myself nets and set them in (a) place suitable, and urge dogs mine so-that wild-animals they chase, until they come to the nets unexpectedly, and so-that they are entangled, and I slay them in the nets.

Nē canst þū huntian būton mid nettum?

Not can you hunt except with nets?

Ġēa, būtan nettum huntian iċ mæġ.

Yes, without nets hunt I can.

Hū?

How?

Mid swiftum hundum iċ betæċe wildēor.

With swift dogs I track wild animals.

Hwilċe wildēor swyþost ġefēhst þū?

Which wild-animals mostly capture you (i.e. do you capture)?

Iċ ġefēo heortas & bāras & rann & rægan & hwīlon haran.

I capture harts and boars and roebucks and goats and sometimes hares.

Wære þū tōdæġ on huntnoþe?

Were you today a-hunting?

Iċ næs, forþām sunnandæġ ys, ac ġyrstandæġ iċ wæs on huntunge.

I was-not, because Sunday (it) is, but yesterday I was a-hunting.

Hwæt ġelæhtest þū?

What captured you (i.e. did you capture)?

Tweġen heortas & ænne bār.

Two harts and one boar.

Hū ġefencge þū hiġ?

How caught you them?

Heortas iċ ġefengc on nettum & bār iċ ofslōh.

(The) harts I caught in nets and (the) boar I slew/struck down.

Hū wære þū dyrstiġ ofstikian bār?

How were you brave (enough) to spear (a) boar?

Hundas bedrifon hyne tō mē, & ic þær tōgēanes standende færlīċe ofstikode hyne.

(The) dogs drove it to me, and I there opposite (i..e. in waiting) standing quickly speared it.

Swyþe þrȳste þū wære þā!

Very brave you were then!

Nē sceal hunta forhtfull wesan, forþām mislīċe wildēor wuniað on wudum.

Not must (a) hunter timid be because (many) different wild-animals live in (the) woods/forest.

Hwæt dēst þū be þīnre huntunge?

What do you with your catch?

Iċ sylle cynce swā hwæt swā iċ ġefō, forþām iċ eom hunta hys.

I give to-the-king whatever I take, because I am hunter his.

Hwæt sylþ hē þē?

What gives he to-you?

Hē scryt mē wel & fētt & hwīlon sylþ mē hors oþþe bēah, þæt þe lustlīcor cræft mīnne iċ begancge.

He clothes me wel and feeds (me) and sometimes gives me (a) hose or (a) precious-ring, so-that by-that more-keenly profession mine I pursue.

from **The Rune Poem**

This is taken by some as important evidence of pre-Christian lore, and certainly the runes and their names were devised prior to and independently of Christian influence. The Rune Poem, however, dates from the Christian period, and is more a literary exercise, with suitably improving comment on each rune name.

Note that Oe poetry does not rhyme. The line structure is provided by alliteration (of consonant with consonant or vowel with any other vowel e.g. in verse 1 the lines alliterate on F, M, D.

F

[Fēoh] byþ frōfur fīra ġehwylcum.
Sceal ðēah manna ġehwylċ miċlun hyt dælan
ġif hē wile for drihtne dōmes hlēotan.

Wealth is (a) consolation of-men to-each.
Much though of-men each much/liberally it deal-out
If he wishes before God merit to-win

U

[Ūr] byþ ānmōd and oferhyrned,
felafreċne dēor, feohteþ mid hornum,
mære mōrstapa; þæt is mōdiġ wuht.

Aurochs is single-minded/staunch and up-horned,
(a) very-fierce beast, (it) fights with (its) horns,
Famed moor-stepper, it is brave creature

TH

[Thorn] byþ ðearle scearp; ðegna ġehwylcum
anfeng ys yfyl, unġemetun rēþe
manna ġehwylcun ðe him mid resteð.

Thorn is greivously sharp; of-thanes/men for-each
Taking-hold is evil, immeasurably painful
Of-men for-each that it upon sits-down

H

[Hæġl] byþ hwītust corna; hwyrft hit of heofones lyfte,
wealcaþ hit windes scūras, weorþeþ hit tō wætere syððan.

Hail is (the) whitest of grains, whirls it from heaven's sky,
Rolls it wind's showers, turns it to water then

I

[Īs] byþ oferċeald, unġemetum slidor,
Glisnaþ glæshlūttur, ġimmum ġelīcust,
flōr forste ġeworuht, fæġer ansyne.

Ice is very-cold, immensely slippery,
it-glistens glass-bright, to-gems most-like,
(a) floor by-frost wrought, fair of-view

S

[Seġel] sēmannum symble biþ on hihte,
ðonn hī hine feriaþ ofer fisces beþ,
oþ hī brimhengest bringeþ tō lande.

(the) sail for-sea-men always is for (a) hope,
When they it carry over fishes' bath (i.e. the sea),
Until them (the) sea-steed (i.e. boat) brings to land.

T

[Tyr] biþ tācna sum, healdeð trywa wel
wiþ æþelingas, ā biþ on færylde
ofer nihta ġenipu, næfre swīċeþ.

The-planet-Mars is of-signs one, holds trust well
with nobles, always is on (the) move
over nights' shadows, never deceives

EO

[Eoh] byþ for eorlum æþelinga wyn,
hors hōfum wlanc, ðær him hæleþ ymbe,
weleġe on wicgum, wrixlaþ spræce,
and biþ unstyllum æfre frōfur.

Horse is for earls (i.e. men) nobles' joy (i.e. a joy to men),
Horse of-hoofs glorious, where him heroes on,
Fortunate on steeds, mingle speech,
And it-is for-the-restless ever (a) consolation

M

[Man] byþ on myrġþe his magan lēof;
sceal þēah ānra ġehwylċ ōðrum swīcan,
for ðām Dryhten wyle dōme sīne
þæt earme flæsc eorþan betæcan.

(the) human is, in mirth, (to) his fellow dear;
must though of-ones each (i.e. evereyone) (the) other betray,
for which God wishes by-decree his
the wretched flesh by-earth to-be-covered (i.e. decrees that all shall die)

Maxims II

There are two poems in OE to which we attribute the title 'Maxims' i.e. sayings or proverbs. So commonplace are most of these, one may suspect a purpose other than that of preserving folk wisdom. As a typical entry ends mid-line, perhaps it formed a sort of word game: a second speaker had to add a new saying, while conforming to the alliteration left in place?

Draca sceal on hlæwe,
frōd, frætwum wlanc. Fisc sceal on wætere
cynren cennan. Cyning sceal on healle
bēagas dælan. Bera sceal on hǣðe,
eald and ēġesfull. Ēa ofdūne sceal
flōdgræġ fēran. Fyrd sceal ætsomne,
tīrfæstra ġetrum. Trēow sceal on eorle,
wīsdom on were. Wudu sceal on foldan
blædum blōwan. Beorh sceal on eorþan

grēne standan. God sceal on heofenum,
dǣda dēmend. Duru sceal on healle,
rūm reċedes mūð. Rand sceal on scylde,
fæst fingra ġebeorh. Fugel uppe sceal
lācan on lyfte. Lēax sceal on wǣle
mid sceote scrīðan. Scūr sceal on heofenum,
winde ġeblanden, in þās woruld cuman.
þēof sceal gangan þystrum wederum. Þyrs sceal on fenne gewunian
āna innan lande.

Dragon must (be) (i.e. belongs) in burial-mound,
Wise, in-treasure proud. Fish must in water
Its kind generate. King must in (a) hall
Rings deal-out. Bear belongs on (the) heath,
Old and full-of-malice. Water downwards must
Flood-grey travel. Army belongs together,
(a) glory-firm company. Trust/loyalty is-proper to (a) warrior,
Wisdom to (a) man. Wood (i.e. tree) must on (the) ground
With-fruits blossom. Grove/woodland must upon (the) earth
Green stand. God belongs in (the) heavens,
Deeds' judger. Door belongs in (a) hall,
Wide rooms' mouth. Round-boss belongs on shield,
Reliable fingers' protection. Bird aloft must
Fly in sky. Salmon must on current
With darting-movement zoom-about. Shower must in (the) heavens,
By-wind mixed-up, into this world come.
Thief must go-about in-darl weathers. Giant must in fenland dwell,
Alone in (the) land.

2. History

The well-known Anglo-Saxon Chronicle in fact consists of several manuscripts, each giving a slightly differen coverage of early English history. Very much aware of their Germanic ancestry, an important starting point for each 'tribe' or kingdom was the time of first settlement and the ancestry of the ruling dynasty.

Parker Chronicle: AD 494 – the founding of Wessex

Þȳ ġēare þe wæs āgān fram Cristes acennesse .cccc. wintra & .xciiii. wintra, þā Cerdic & Cynric his sunu cuōm ūp æt Cerdicesoran mid .v. scipum; & se Cerdic wæs Elesing, Elesa Esling, Esla Gewising, Giwis Wiging, Wig Freawining, Freawine Friþugaring, Friþugar Bronding,

Brond Bældæging, Bældæg Wodening. Ond þæs ymb .vi. ġēar þæs þe hīe ūp cuomon, ġe-ēodon Westsēaxna rīċe, & þæt wǣrun þā ǣrestan cyningas þe Westsēaxna lond on Wealum ġe-ēodon; & hē hæfde þæt rīċe .xvi. ġēar, & þā hē ġefōr, þā feng his sunu Cynric tō þām rīċe & heold .xvii. winter.

In-the year which was past from Christ's birth 400 winters and 94 winters, then Cerdic and Cynric his son came up (i.e. landed) at Cerdic's Beach with 5 ships; and that Cerdic was Elesa's son, Elesa Esla's son, Esla Giwis' son, Giwis Wig's son, Wig Freawine's son, Freawine Grithusgar's son, Frithugar Brond's son, Brond Bældæg's son, Bældæg Woden's son. And after about 6 years after they landed, they-established (the) West Saxons' kingdom, and that/they were the first kings that West Saxons' land among (the) Welsh/British established; and he had (i.e. tuled) that kingdom 16 years, and when the passed-on, then succeeded his son Cynric to the kingdom and held (it) 17 winters (i.e. years).

AD 793 – the arrival of the Vikings (from BL Ms Cotton Tiberius B.iv). This is one of the turning points for English history – especially for the North of England, told in terms of a (super)natural and as well as political diasaster.

Hēr wǣron rēðe forebēcna cumene ofer Norðhymbra land, and þæt folc earmliċ breġdon, þæt wǣron ormete þodenas and līġ-rescas, and fyrenne dracan wǣron ġesewene on þām lifte flēoġende.

Here were harsh forewarning-sings come over Northumbrian's land, and the folk/people wretched terrified, that were huge storms and lightning-flashes, and fiery dragons were seen in the sky, flying.

Þām tācnum sōna fyliġde myċel hunger, and litel æfter þām, þæs ilcan ġēares on vi Idus Ianuarii, earmlīċe hæþenra manna hergunc ādilegode Godes ċyriċan in Lindisfarnaee þurh hrēaf-lāc and mansliht

(Upon) Those tokens/signs at-once followed (a) great famine, and (a) little after that, in-the same year, on (the) 6th (day before the) Ides of January, wretchedly heathen men's army destroyed God's church in Lindisfrane with raiding and slaughter.

Parker Chronicle AD 878 – Alfred's victory at Ethandun

Hēr hiene bestæl se here on midne winter ofer tuelftan niht to Ċippanhamme, & ġerīdon Wessēaxna lond & ġesǣton & miċel þæs folċes ofer sæ ā-drǣfdon, & þæs ōþres þone mǣstan dǣl hīe ġerīdon, & him tō ġecirdon būton þām cyninge Ælfrede. & hē lytle werede unīeþelīċe æfter wudum fōr, & on mōrfæstenum...

Here (i.e. in this year) sneaked the (Viking) army at mid winter on Twelfth Night to Chippenham (Alfred's headquarters), and overran (the) West-Saxons' land and occupied (it) and many of-the folk over sea they-drove, and of-the rest the most part they (i.e. the Vikings) made-submit and them to turned except the king Alfred and he with (a) little troop...

& þæs ilcan wintra wæs Inwæres brōþur & Healfdenes on Westsēaxum on Defenascīre mid .xxiii. scipum, & hiene mon þær ofslōg, & .dccc. monna mid him. & .xl. monna his heres; & þæs on Eastron worhte Ælfred cyning lytle werede ġeweorc æt Æþelinga-ēigge, & of þām ġeweorċe was winnende wiþ þone here, & Sumursætna se dæl, se þǣr nīehst wæs;

And (in) the same winter was (i.e. went) Inwær's brother and Healdene's in Wessex in Devonshire with 23 ships, and him someone there slew, and 900 men [auxiliaries? Celts?] with him, and 40 men of-his army; and afterwards at Easter built Alfred (the) king with (a) little company (an) earthwork at Athelney, and from that stronghold was contending with the (Viking) army, and (him helped) of-the-Seomerset-folk that part, that (to) there nearest was.

Þā on þǣre seofoðan wiecan ofer Eastron hē ġerād tō Ecgbryhtes stāne be ēastan Sealwyda, & him tō cōmon þǣr onġēn Sumorsæte alle, & Wilsætan, & Hamtunscīr se dǣl se hiere behinon sǣ wæs, & his ġefæġene wǣrun; & hē fōr ymb āne niht of þām wīcum to Iglea, & þæs ymb āne tō Eþandune, & þǣr ġefeaht wiþ alne þone here, & hiene ġefliemde, & him æfter rād oþ þæt ġeweorc, & þǣr sæt .xiiii. niht;

Then in the seventh week after Easter he (Alfred) rode to Echbryht's Stone to-the east of-Selwood, and him to came there towards Somerset-men all, and (the) Wiltshire-men, and Hamptonshire the part that -- within (the) sea was [i.e. not the Isle of Wight]. And (to see) him (i.e. Alfred) glad they-were; and he travelled over one night from the campsites to Iley, and then after one (night) to Ethandun, and there fought with all the (Viking) army, and them put-to-flight, and them afterwards pursued up-to that (i.e. the Vikings') earthwork, and there sat (i.e. besieged them) (for) 14 nights(i.e. days).

& þā salde se here him fore-ġīslas & miċle āþas þæt hīe of his rīċe woldon & him ēac ġehēton þæt kyning fulwihte onfōn wolde & hīe þæt gelǣston swā, & þæs ymb .iii. wiecan cōm se cyning tō him Godrum þritiga sum þāra monna þe in þām here weorþuste wǣron æt Alre, & þæt is wiþ Æþelingga-eige; & his se cyning þǣr onfeng æt fulwihte, & his crismlising was æt Weþmor, & he wæs .xii. niht mid þām cyninge, & hē hine miċlum & his ġefēran mid fēo weorðude.

And then gave the (Viking) army to-him (i.e. Alfred) hostages and great oaths that they from his kingdom would (go) and to-him also promised that (the Viking) king baptism to-receive wished and they that performed just-so, and then after 3 weeks came the king to him Gudrum (i.e. King Gudrum came to Alfred) of-thirty one (i.e. one of a party of 30) of-the-men that in that (Viking) army most-statused were, at Aller, and that is by Athelney; and him the king (Alfred) there received in baptism, and his (Gudrum's) completion was at Wedmore, and he was 12 nights (i.e. days) with the king; and he (Alfred) him (gudrun) greatly and his companions with wealth honoured.

William I (ASC 1100)

Hē wæs on ġītsunge befeallan & grǣdiġnæsse hē lufode mid eallan.
Hē sætte myċel dēor-frīð & hē læġde laga þǣrwið þæt swā hwā swā slōge heort oððe hinde þæt hine man sceolde blendian. Hē forbēad þā heortas swylċe ēac þā bāras. Swā swīðe hē lufode þā hēa-dēor swylċe hē wǣre heora fæder. Ēac hē sætte be þǣm haran þæt hī mōsten frēo faran. His rīċe men hit mǣndon & þā earme men hit be-ċeorodan. Ac he wæs swā stīð þæt hē ne rōhte heora eallra nīð, ac hī mōston mid ealle þes cynges wille folgian ġif hī woldon libban oððe land habban land oððe eahta oððe wel his sehta. Wālāwā!

He was into covetousness fallen and acquisition he loved above all. He established an extensive monopoly on deer and laid down laws about it so that whoever slew a hart or a hind -- him one must blind. He forbade (common use of) deer and likewise of boars. So intensely he loved the tall deer as if he was their father. Also he established for hares that they be-allowed free to-roam. His barons it regretted and the humble men of-it complained but he was very unyielding so that he not regarded all their hostility, but they must entirely this king's wishes follow – if they would live or landed-estate retain – land or honours or even his goodwill. Alas!

Athelstan defeats the Vikings at Brunanburh

Also from the Chronicle comes a poem celebrating the Anglo-Saxon victory over a Viking conferacy in 937 AD (Anlaf and Constantine). That Wessex was ruled by three successive very competent kings – Alfred, Edward and Athelstan – is one reason that it was able to expand to form a state very similar in extent to modern England; equally the Vikings had in many cases integrated within an agricultural and trading society and had little reason to continue an armed struggle.

At the end of this battle poem is a striking image of 'the beasts of battle' feeding on the dead left on the field.

Ġewīton him þā North-menn naeġled-cnearrum,
Departed – the (or then) Northmen (i.e. Vikings) in-nailed-ships
drēorig daroða lāf, on dinges mere
dreary spears' remant (i.e.surviors), on ?stormy/dark sea
ofer dēop waeter Dyflin sēcan,
over deep water Dublin to-seek
eft Iraland aewisc-mōde.
back to-Ireland feint-hearted
Swelċe þā ġebrōðor bēġen aetsamne,
Similarly the brothers both together,
cyning and aeþeling, cyððe sōhton,
(the) king and prince (i.e.Athelstan and Edmund)), homeland sought,
Westsēaxna land, wīġes hremġe.
Westsaxons' land, in-victory exultant.
Lēton him behindan hrǣw bryttian
They-left them behind (the) corpses to-dispose-of
sealwiġ-padan, þone sweartan hraefn
dark-coat, the black raven
hyrned-nebban, and þone hasu-padan,
horn-beaked, and the grey-coat,
earn aeftan hwīt, ǣses brucan,
(the) eagle posteriorly white,the-food to-use,
grædiġne gūð-hafoc, and þaet græġe dēor,
(and the) greedy war-hawk, and the grey beast
wulf on wealda.
wolf in forest.

3. Heroic Literature

The Fight at Finnsburh

This leads us appropriately to the heroic literature that survives, fantastic and blood-curdling enough ot satisfy the most credulous of Christian audiences. The first example survives only as a fragment, reporting the death of Finn, besieged by Hnæf the Frisian while Finn was a guest of Hnæf's. (Later he is avenged by Hengest.)

Here Hnæf awakens to the sound and torch-light of a night attack:

Hnæf hlēoþrode ðā, heaþo-ġeong cyning:

Hnæf spoke then, war-young king:

"Nē ðis ne dagað ēastan, nē hēr draca ne fleoġeð,

"Not this dawns from-the-east, nor here dragon flies,

nē hēr ðisse healle hornas ne byrnað.

Nor heer this hall's horns/gables burn,

Ac hēr forþ berað; fugelas singað,

But here forward they-advance (i.e. attackers): birds sing,

ġylleð græġ-hama, gūð-wudu hlynneð,

yells (the) grey-coat (i.e. eagle), war-wood (?shields) bangs,

scyld scefte oncwyð. Nū scyneð þes mōna

shield to-shaft/spear echoes. Now shines this moon

wāðol under wolcnum. Nū ārīsað wēa-dǣda

wandering under sky. Now arise bad-deeds

ðe ðisne folċes nīð fremman willað.

that (to?) this people harm do will/intend.

Ac onwacnigeað nū, wīġend mīne,

But wake-up now, warriors mine,

habbað ēowre linda, hicgeaþ on ellen,

have/hold your linden-shields, think on bravery,

winnað on orde, wesað ōnmōde!"...

fight in format, be resolute!"...

The OE Alexander: Alexander thirsty

Though it evidences the Anglo-Saxon love of marvels and exotic tales, the OE Alexander is not an original composition but derived from a Latin (and ultimately a Greek) 'novel'. This tells of Alexander's campaigns in the East, until he reaches India. There he consults prophetic trees, only to learn that they predict he will never live to return home – a sad climax to the many adventures and acts of heroism marking the journey eastwards.

Þā ġelomp us þæt wē wurdon earfōðlīċe mid þurste ġeswencte & ġewæcte. Ðone þurst wē þonne earfōðlīċe ābǣron & ārǣfndon, þā wæs hāten Seferus mīn þeġn funde þā wæter in ānum holan stāne & þā mid āne

helme hlōd hit & mē tō brōhte. And hē sylfa þursti wæs se mīn þeġn, &
hwæþre hē swīðor mīnes fēores & ġesynto wilnade þonne his selfes.

*Then it-happened to-us that we were terribly with thirst afflicted and
weakened. That thirst we then with-hardship bore and endured, when
(someone) was called Severus, my thane, found then water in an hollow
stone, and then with a helmet loaded it and me to brought (it). And he
himself thirsty was he my thane, and yet he more-greatly for-my life and
health wished than of-his own.*

Þā hē þā þæt wæter mē tō brōhte swā iċ ær sæġde, þā hēt iċ mīn weorod
& ealle mīne duguþe tōsomne, & hit þā beforan heora ealra onsyne niðer
āġēat, þy læs iċ drunce & þone mīnne þeġn þyrste & mīnne here & ealne
þe mid me wæs. Ond iċ þā beforan him eallum herede Seferes dæde þæs
mīnes þeġnes, & hine beforan hiora ealra onsīone mid dēor-weorðum
ġyfum ġeġeafede for ðære dæde.

*When he then that water me to brought as I before said, then ordered I my
troop and all my company (to come) together, and it then before of-them
all (the) sight downward poured, the less I should-drink and him my thane
thirst and my army and everyone that with me was. And I then before
them all praised Severus for-the dead of-him my thane, and him before of-
them all (the) sight with precious gifts endowed for that deed.*

Beowulf: Beowulf's funeral

Ġeworhton ðā Wedra lēode

Wrought then (the) Weders' people

Hlǣw on hlīðe, sē wæs hēah ond brād,

mound on headland that was high and broad,

wæg-līðendum wīde ġesȳne,

to-wave-travellers widely visible

ond betimbredon on tȳn dagum

and constructed in ten days

beadu-rōfes bēcn, bronda lāfe

*war-brave-one's (i.e. Beowulf's) monument, flames' remnant (i.e.
Beowulf's ashes)*

wealle beworhton, swā hyt weorðlīcost

with-a-wall surrounded, as it best

fore-snotre men findan mihton.
Most-wise men devise could.
Hī on beorg dydon bēg ond siglu,
They into mound did (i.e. put) rings and jewels,
eall swylċe hyrsta, swylċe on horde ǣr
also trasures, such-as on (dragon's) hoard earlier
nīð-hēdiġe men ġenumen hæfdon,
fierce-minded men plaed had.
forlēton eorla ġestrēon eorðan healdan,
they-abandoned warriors' treasure for-the-earth to hold,
gold on grēote, þær hit nū ġēn lifað
gold in (the) ground, there it now still surives
eldum swā unnyt swā hit ǣror wæs.
To-men as useless as it before was.
Þā ymbe hlæw riodan hilde-dīore,
Then around mound rode battle-keen-ones
æþelinga bearn, ealra twelfe,
princes' sons, in-all twelve,
woldon care cwīðan ond kyning mǣnan,
wished sorrow to-voice and(their) king to-mourn,
word-ġyd wrecan ond ymb wer sprecan;
word-song to-make and about (the) man to-speak;
eahtodan eorlscipe ond his ellen-weorc
they-pondered (his) courage and his brave-deeds
duguðum dēmdon, swā hit ġedēfe bið
(his) merits they-assessed, as it fitting is
þæt mon his wine-dryhten wordum herġe,
that anyone his dear-lord in-words praise,
ferhðum frēoge, þonne hē forð scile

qualities-of-mind honour, when he forth must
of līċ-haman læded weorðan.
From body-coating led be (i.e. die).

Swā begnornodon Ġēata lēode
Thus bemourned Geats' people,
hlāfordes hryre, heorð-ġenēatas,
(their) lord's fall, (his) hearth-men:
cwædon þæt he wære wyruld-cyninga
they-said that he was of-world-kings
manna mildust ond mon-ðwærust,
of-men the) most-mild (i.e. merciful) and sociable,
lēodum līðost ond lof-ġeornost.
To-his-people most-generous and most-keen-for-praise.

4. Laws & Charters
From The Preface to Alfred's Laws

Iċ ðā, Ælfred cyning, þās tōgædere ġegaderode & āwrītan hēt, moneġe þāra þe ūre fore-gengan heoldon, ðā ðe mē līcodon; & maneġe þāra þe mē ne līcodon iċ āwearp mid mīnra witena ġeðeahte, & on ōðre wīsan bebēad tō healdanne.

I, the, Alfred, king, these together gathered and written-down ordered: many of those which our predecessors held/observed, which to-me appealed; and many of those which to-me not appealed, I cast-aside with my witans' (Council's) agreement, and in another wise/form ordered to be-held/observed.

Forðām iċ ne dorste ġeðristlæcan þāra mīnra āwuht fela on ġewrit settan, forðām mē wæs uncūð, hwæt þæs ðām līcian wolde ðe æfter us wæren.

For-this-reason I not dared to-be-so-prreseumptious (as) of-those my-own anything much in writing to set-down, because toi-me it-was unknowable, what later to-them please would that after us would-be.

Ac ðā ðe iċ ġemette āwðer oððe on Ines dæġe, mīnes mæġes, oððe on Offan Mercna cyninges oððe on Æþelbryhtes, þe ærest fulluhte onfēng on Angelcynne, þā ðe me ryhtoste ðūhton, iċ þā hēr-on ġegaderode, & þā

39

ōðre forlēt. Ić ðā Ælfred Westsēaxna cyning eallum mīnnum witum þās ġe-ēowde, & hīe ðā cwædon þæt him þæt līcode eallum tō healdanne.

But those that I met/encountered either in Ine's day/time – my kinsman – or in Offa's – (the Mercians' king – or in Æthelbryht's, who first baptism received in English-kin (i.e. nation), those that to-me most-proper seemed, I them herein gathered, and the others abandoned. I then, Alfred, West-Saons' king, to all my Witan (Counsellors) these showed, and they then said that to-them it pleased all-of-them to be-observed.

Alfred's Laws ch. 43

It was assumed at this time, that in an observant society, it was not so much a matter of fixing guilt as of setting penalties. To kill someone in fair fight was not so much a crime as a public fact for which recompense must be paid to the victim's kin. But to kill someone secretly – *morðor* – was to 'murder' them, and the penalty was hanging. (This distinction remains in place today, between murder and manslaughter.) For lesser injuries, a tariff was set out.

Note: *man* in this text is used impersonally, as it is in German, where we would say 'one does something…'

Ġif mon men ēaġe of-āslēa, ġeselle him mon .lx. scillinga & .vi. scillinga & .vi. pæningas & ðriddan dǣl pæninges tō bōte.

If one someone's eye knocks-out, shall-give to-him (i.e. the victim) (the) doer 60 shillings and six shillings and six pennies and (the) third part of-a-penny as booty/recompense.

Ġif hit in ðām heafde sīe, & hē nōht ġesēon ne mæġe mid, stande ðriddan dǣl þǣre bōte inne.

If it in the head be (i.e. remains), and/but he not see can with-it, (a) third part of-the recompense (be) held-back.

Ġif mon ōðrum þæt neb of-āslēa, ġebēte him mid .lx. scillingum.

If someone to-another the nose cut-off, recompense him with 60 shillings.

Ġif mon ōðrum ðone tōð onforan heafde of-āslēa, ġebēte þæt mid .viii. scillingum.

If one to-another the tooth in-the-front-of (the) head knock-out, recompense that with 8 shillings.

Ġif hit sīe se wong-tōð, ġeselle .iii. scillinga tō bōte. Monnes tux bið .xv. scillinga weorð.

If it be the cheek-tooth (i.e. a molar), three shillings as recompnse. (A) man's tusk (i.e. eye-tooth, or canine) 16 shillings' value.

Ine's Laws ch. 87

Ðonne mon bēam on wuda forbærne, & weorðe yppe on þone ðe hit dyde, ġielde hē ful-wīte: ġeselle .lx. scillinga; forþāmþe fȳr bið þēof. Ġif mon āfelle on wuda wel monega trēowa, & wyrð eft undierne, for-ġielde .iii. trēowu ǣlċ mid .xxx. scillingum; nē ðearf hē hiora mā ġeldan, wǣre hiora swā fela swa hiora wǣre, forþon sīo æsc bið melda, nālles ðēof.

If someone (a) tree in (a) forest burn-down and it-is proved on him that it did, yield he full-fine: let-him-give 60 shillings, because fire is (a) thief (i.e. a form of theft). If one fell in (a)forest very many trees, and it-is afterwards obvious (who did it), let-him-pay (for) three trees each with 30 shillings; not need he for-them more pay, were-it of-them (i.e. the doers?) as many as of-them (the trees?) it-were, because the ax is (an) intermediary not (a) thief.

Charters

Charters conventionally have three parts: the declaration of the grants in Latin, a note of the bounds (often in Ol d English) and the signatures of witnesses (usually a mark or cross, with the name written in by the scribe). Charters defined *bōcland* (bookland, land in priavte ownership) as opposed to folk-land or common land.

Grant of privileges of AD 924 x 939 of King Athelstan to St Paul's minster.

In this example, unusually, the declaration itself in in Old English. Regarded by some commentators as spurious (i.e. a fake) it is nonetheless interesting evidence of a valid tradition of how St Paul's was founded.

On þām hālgan naman ūres hālendes Cristes sē þe us ġescōp þā þe sylfe nǣron & us eft ālȳsde mid his āgenum līfe þā þā fordone wǣron þurh þaes dēofles lāre & mid ealle for-scylgode into þām ēcan sūsle, ac his myċċle ārfæstnese us ālȳsde of ðām.

In the holy name of-our saviour Christ, he that us created when (we) (our)selves were-not (i.e. were nothing?), and us then redeemed with his own life, when undone we-were through the Devil's teaching and entirely condemned to the eternal torment, but by-his large mercy us he-freed of that.

Nū iċ Aðelstan cyning ofer Ængla þēode cȳþe mīnum witum & on þisum ġewrite mid wordum āfæstniġe þæt iċ wille friðian ealle þā lande are into S. Paules mynstre & þæretō ġesetan þysne *priuilege* þæt is synderliċ frēols S. Paul tō lofe, þan hālgan apostle þe þēos stōw is hāliġ, mīnre sāule tō ālysednesse & mīne synnan tō forġifenesse, be þām þe Sybba cyng hit ġefrēode & se hālga Erkenwold

Now I, Athelstan, king over (the) Angles' nation, make-known to-my witan / counsellors and on this writ with words confirm that I wish to-free (of any imposition) all those lands [that are?] to St Paul's Minster and thereto establish this privilege, which is (a) special independence, (of) St Paul in praise, the holy apostle that this place is hallowed to, for-my soul as redemption and to-my sins as forgiveness, ?in the (same) way that Sibba (the) king it [first] made-free and the holy Erconwald.

Grant of A.D. 739 by King Æthelheard of Wessex of an estate at Crediton, Devon.

Bounds are often difficult to translate as they involve many local peculiarities. The following sample is notable for containing a reference to Grendel, the villain of the Beowulf poem.

Ærest of cridian brycge on herpað . andlanges herpaðes on sulhford to exan . þonne andlang eaxan oð focgan iġeðas . of focgan iġeðum on landsceare hricg . of landsceare hricge on luhan trēow . of luhan trēowe on hagan get . of hagan gate on doddan hrycg . of doddan hrycge on grendeles pyt . of grendeles pytte on ifiġbearo . of ifiġbeara on hrucgan cumbes ford . of hrucgan cumbes forda on fearnburh . of fearnbyrig on earnes hricg... .

First from ?Crediton Bridge on (the) army-path; along (the) army-path at ?plough-ford to the Exe. Then along (the) Exe as-far-as (the) grassy eyots; from (the) grassy eyots to (the) boundary ridge; from (the) boundary ridge to (the) ?lake's tree; from (the) ?lake's tree to the hedge gate; from (the) hedge gate to ?bare ridge; from (the) ?bare ridge to Grendel's pit; from Grendel's pit to (the) ivy grove; from (the) ivy grove to ridge's valley's ford; from ridge's valley's ford to (the) ferny-hill; from (the) ferny-hill to (the) eagle's ridge...

Another administrative tool was the writ, by which the King conveyed an order to specific people – a positive action (whereas laws by definition are negative).

Here William the Conqueror reassures the citizens of London that he will be even-handed to Norman and Anglo-Saxon alike....

Will[ia]m kyng grēt Will[ia]m bisceop and Gosfreġð portirēfan and ealle þā burhwaru binnan Londone, frenċisce and englisce, frēondlīċe. And iċ kūðe ēow þæt iċ wylle þæt ġēt bēon eallre þæra laga weorðe þe ġȳt wæran on Eadweardes dæġe kynges; and iċ wylle þæt ǣlċ ċyld bēo his fāder yrfnume æfter his fæder dæġe, and iċ nelle geþolian þæt ǣniġ man ēow ǣniġ wrang bēode. God ēow ġehealde.

William (the) king greets William (the) bishop and Gosfrith (the) portreeve and all the citizens in London, French and English, in-friendly-manner. And I make-known to-you that I wish that still shall< be (i.e. apply) all of-those laws [<shall] that formerly were [observed] in Edward's day/lifetime, the king, and I will that each child shall-be his father's heir after his father's day/lifetime, and I will not allow that any man to-you any wrong shall-offer. God you preserve!

5. The Church

from Psalm 83:

Synd mē wīċ þīne weorðe and lēofe,
Are to-me dwellings yours admirable and dear,

mæġena drihten; ā iċ on mōde þæs
of-powers Lord; ever I in mind of-that

willum hæfde, þet iċ him wunude onn.
gladly had, that I them might-dwell in.

Heorte mīn and flæsc hyhtað ġeorne
Heart mine and flesh trust keenly

on þone līfiġendan lēofan drihten;
in the living dear God.

him ēac spēdlīċe spearuwa hūs beġyteð,
for-himself also successfully sparrow house makes

and tīdlīċe turtle nistlað,
and in-season the-turtle-dove does-nest

þær hīo āfēdeð fugelas ġeonge.
where she feeds birds young.

Wærun wiġ-bedu þīn, weoruda drihten;
Were-they altars yours, of-hosts Lord;

þū eart drihten mīn and dēore cynincg.
you are God mine and dear king.

Ēadiġe weorðað, þā þe eardiað
Blessed they-are, who dwell

on þīnum hūsum, hāliġ drihten,
in your houses, holy Lord,

and þe on worulda woruld, wealdend, heriað.
And you for worlds' world (i.e. for ever), Ruler, praise.

The Lord's Prayer

Ēalā ūre fæder þe on heofonum eart,
Lo! Our Father that in (the) heavens are

ā sȳ ðīn nama ēċelīċe ġeblētsod.
ever be your name eternally blessed.

& ðīn rīċedom ofer us rīxie symble,
and your kingdom over us rule always,

& ðīn willa ġewyrðe
and your will come-to-pass

swā swā on heofonum ēac swā on eorðan.
as in (the) heavens so-too on earth.

Ġe-unn us tō þissum dæġe dæġ-hwāmlīċes fōstres.
Grant us for this day (our) daily food.

And us ġemildsa swā swā wē miltsiað
And us be-merciful-to as we show-mercy

þām ðe wið us āġyltaþ;
to-them that against us are-guilty.

& ne læt ðū us costnian ealles tō swȳðe,
and not let you us be-tempted entirely too strongly,

ac ālȳs us fram yfele, amen.
but free us from evil, Amen.

From the WS Gospels...

Biddaþ & ēow bið ġeseald. Sēċeaþ & ġē hit findaþ. Cnuciað & ēow biþ ontȳned.

Ask and to-you it-will-be given. Seek and you it will-find. Knock and to-you it-will-be opened.

Witodlīċe ǣlċ þǣra þe bit, hē onfehþ; & sē þe sēċð, hē hyt fint; & þām cnuċiendum, bið ontȳned.

Assuredly, each of-them that asks, he will-receive; and he that seeks, he it will-find; and to-the (person) knocking, it-will-be opened.

Hwylċ man is of ēow ġyf his sunu hyne bit hlāfes sylst þū him stān, oððe ġyf he bytt fisces sylst þū him næddran?

Which one is from-among you if his son him asks for-bread give you him (a) stone, or if he asks for-fish give you him (an) adder (i.e. snake)?

Eornustlīċe nū ġē þe yfle synt cunnun gōde sylena ēowrum bearnum syllan, myċle mā ēower Fæder þe on heofenum ys syleþ gōd þām þe hyne biddað.

Truly now (if?) you that evil are can good gifts to-your children give, much more your Father that in (the) heavens is will-give good to-them who him ask.

6. Saints' Lives

from Ælfric's Life of Cuthbert

Þēs foresǣda hālga wer wæs ġewunod þæt hē wolde gān on niht tō sǣ

This aforesaid holy man (C) was accustomed that he would go at night to (the) sea

and standan on ðām sealtan brymme oð his swȳran syngende his ġebcdu.

and stand in the salty ocean upto his neck singing his devotions.

Þā on sumere nihte hlosnode sum ōðer munuc his fǣreldes

Then on one night spied some other monk on-his journey

and mid sleaċċre stalcunge his fōt-swāðum filiġde

and with stealthy pace his footsteps followed

oðþæt hī beġen tō sǣ becōmon.

until they both to (the) sea came.

Ðā dyde Cūþberhtus swā his ġewuna wæs,

Then did Cuthbert as his custom was,

sang his ġebedu on sǣlīċere ȳðe, standende oð þone swȳran

sang his prayers in marine waves, standing upto the neck

and sȳððan his cnēowa on ðām ċeosle ġebiġde,

and then his knees on the sand he-bent,

āstrehtum hand-brēdum tō heofenlīcum rodore.

with-stretched palms to (the) heavenly sky.

Efne ðā cōmon tweġen sēolas of sǣlicum grunde

Just then came two seals from marine depth

and hī mid heora flȳse his fēt dryġdon

and they with their fur his feet dried

and mid heora blǣde his lēoma bēðedon,

and with their breath his limbs warmed,

and sīððan mid ġebēacne his blētsunge bǣdon,

and then with gesture his blessing sought,

licgende æt his fōton on fealwum ċeosle.

lying at his feet on (the) yellow sand.

Þā Cūðberhtus ðā sǣlican nytenu

Then Cuthbert the marine animals

on sund āsende mid sōðre blētsunge

into (the) deep sent with true blessing

and on meriġenlīċere tīde mynster ġesōhte.

and at dawning time (the) monastery regained.

Edmund's Head

Hwæt ðā se flot-here fērde eft tō scipe,

Well then the sea-army (i.e. Vikings) went back to ship.

and behȳddon þæt heafod þæs hālgan Eadmundes

and hid the head of-the holy Edmund

on þām þiċċum bremelum þæt hit bebyrġed ne wurde.
On the thick brambles that it buried not could-be.

Þā æfter fyrste, syððan hī āfarene wǣron,
Then after (a) while, when they gone were,

cōm þæt land-folc tō þe þǣr tō lāfe wæs þā,
came the local-folk back who there as remainder was then,

þǣr heora hlāfordes līċ læġ būtan heafde,
where their lord's body lay without (its) head.

and wurdon swīðe sāriġe for his sleġe on mōde,
and they-were very unhappy on-account-of his slaying in (their) mind(s),

and hūrū þæt hī næfdon þæt heafod tō þām bodiġe.
And especially that they had-not the head (belonging) to the body.

Þā sǣde se sceawere þe hit ǣr ġesēah
Then said the witness who it earlier saw

þæt þā flot-men hæfdon þæt heafod mid him,
that the flett-men had (taken) that head with them,

and wæs him ġeðūht swā swā hit wæs ful sōð
and it-did to-him seem, as it was quite true,

þæt hī behȳddon þæt heafod on þām holte for-hwēga.
That they hid the head on the forest somewhere.

Hī ēodon þā sēċende ealle endemes tō þām wuda,
they went then seeking, all, together to the forest,

sēċende ġehwǣr ġeond þȳfelas and bremelas
seeking everywhere among bushes and brambles

ġif hī āhwǣr mihton ġemeton þæt heafod.
In-case they anywhere could discover the head.

Wæs ēac miċel wundor þæt ān wulf wearð āsend,
Was also (a) great marvel that a wolf was sent

þurh Godes wissunge tō beweriġenne þæt heafod
through God's direction to guard the head
wið þā ōþre dēor, ofer dæġ and niht.
Against the other wild-animals, over day and night.
Hī ēodon þā sēċende, and symle clypiġende,
they went then searching, and continually calling-out
swā swā hit ġewuneliċ is þām ðe on wuda gāð oft,
as it customary is for-them who in woodland go often,
"Hwǣr eart þū nū ġefēra?" And him andwyrde
'Where are you now friend?' And to-them answered
þæt heafod, "Hēr, hēr, hēr;"
the head, 'Here, here, here!'.
and swā ġelōme clypode
and as often called-out,
andswariġende him eallum, swā oft swā heora ǣniġ clypode,
answering to-them all, as often as of-them any called-out,
oþþæt hī ealle becōmen þurh ðā clypunga him tō.
Until they all came through the calling-out it to.
Þā læġ se grǣga wulf þe bewiste þæt heafod,
Then (?there) lay the grey wolf that protexted the head
and mid his twām fōtum hæfde þæt heafod beclypped,
and with his two feet had the head embraced,
grǣdiġ and hungriġ, and for Gode ne dorste
greedy and hungry, and (yet) for God not dared
þæs heafdes ābȳrian, and heold hit wið dēor.
Of-the-head to-taste, and (i..e. but) protected it against wild-animals
Þā wurdon hī ofwundrode þæs wulfes hyrd-rǣdenne,
Then were they astonsihed at-the wolf's guardianship

and þæt hāliġe heafod hām feredon mid him,
and the holy head home carried with them,
þanciġende þām ælmihtigan ealra his wundra;
thanking to-the Almighty for-all his wonders,
ac se wulf folgode forð mid þām heafde
and/but the wolf followed forward with the head
oþþæt hi tō tūne cōmon, swylce hē tām wǣre,
until they to town came, as-if he tame were,
and ġewende eft sīþþan tō wuda onġēan.
And departed back then to (the) forest once-more.

7. Science

From Byrthferth's Manual – a calculation designed to identify the *bisextus* or leap-year.

Efne seofon bēoð sufon

Just seven is seven

twīa seofon bēoð fēowertȳne

twice 7 is 14

þrīwa seofon bēoð ān & twentiġ

thrice 7 is 21

fēower sīðon seofon bēoð eahta & twentiġ

$4 \times 7 = 28$

fīf sīðon seofon bēoð fīf & þrittiġ

$5 \times 7 = 35$

syx sīðon seofon bēoð twā & fēowertiġ

$6 \times 7 = 42$

seofon sīðon seofon bēoð nigon & fēowertiġ

$7 \times 7 = 49$

eahta sīðon seofon bēoð syx & fīftiġ

8 x 7 = 56

nigon sīðon seofon bēoð þrēo & syxtiġ

9 x 7 = 63

tȳn sīðon seofon bēoð hund-seofontiġ

10 x 7 = 70

twentiġ sīðon seofon bēoð ān hund & fēowertiġ

20 x 7 = 140

þrittiġ sīðon seofon bēoð twā hundred & tȳn

30 x 7 = 210

fēowertiġ sīðon seofon bēoð twā hundred & hund-eahtatiġ

40 x 7 = 280

fīftiġ sīðon seofon bēoð þrēo hundred & fīftiġ

50 x 7 = 350

Ġīt þǣr synt fīftēne tō lāfe

Yet there are fifteen as remainder

tōdǣlað þā eall swā þā ōðre

divide them just like the others

twīa seofon bēoð fēowertȳne

2 x 7 = 14

Nū þǣr ys ān tō lāfe

Now there is one as remainder

nim þæt ān & sete on foreweardum þām *concurrentium*, & cweð *primus cum bissexto.*

Take that one and put (it) before the 'concurrent', and call (it) 'primus cum bissexto'

Note: hund-seofontiġ, hund-eahtatiġ, not 170, 180, but 70, 80 i.e. seventy-in-the vicinity-of-a-hundred, etc.

The OE Boethius: The elements of earth and water

To King Alfred is attributed a tranlsation into OE of the philosophical writings of the Roman, Boethius. In Metre 20, he expounds a simple precursor of gravity. The four elements have distinct positions: fire uppermost, then air, then water and earth supporting the rest. Each aspires to return to its home, thus fire flares upwards, and water topples downwards. But they can also mix...

Hwæt, þū þǣm wættere wætum & ċealdum

Lo!, you for-the water wet and cold

foldan tō flōre fæste ġesettest

the-earth as (a) floor firmly estalished

forðǣm hit unstille ǣġ-hwider wolde

because it (i.e. water) un-still/restless everywhere would

wīde tō-scrīðan, wāc & hnesce:

widely run-away, weak and soft:

nē meahte hit on him selfum (sōð iċ ġēare wāt)

not could it in its self – sooth/truth I clearly know –

ǣfre ġestandan ac hit sīo eorðe hȳlt

ever stand/stay-in-place but it the earth holds

& swelġeð ēac be sumum dǣle

and swallows/absorbs also to some/a-certain extent

þæt hīo sīðþan mæġ for ðǣm sype weorðan

that she(i.e. the earth) then can through the soaking become

ġeleht lyftum: forðǣm lēaf & gærs

moistened by-the-clouds: wherefore leaf/foliage and grass

brǣd ġeond Bretene, blōweð & grōweð

spreads yond/across Britain, blooms and grows

eldum tō āre: eorðe sīo ċealde

for-men as a-benefit: earth the cold

brengð wæstma fela wundorlīcra,
brings-forth crops' many wonderful,

forðǣm hīo mid þǣm wætere weorðað ġeþāwened:
because it with the water was moistened:

ġif þæt nǣre, þonne hīo wǣre
if that was-not, then it (earth) would-be

for-drugod tō dūste & tōdrifen sīððan
dried-out to dust and driven-about then

wīde mid winde, swā nū weorðað oft
widely with (the) wind, as now happens often,

axe ġiond eorðan eall tōblāwen:
ashes around the-earth/world all blown-about

nē meahte on ðǣre eorðan āwuht libban
nor could on the earth anything live.

8. Medicine

þā ealdan lǣċas ġesettan on ledenbōcun, þæt on ǣlcum mōnðe bēoð ǣfre tweġen dagas, þe syndan swȳðe deriġendlīċe ǣniġne drenċ on tō ðicgenne, oððe blōd on tō lǣtenne, forðan þe ān tīd is on ǣlcum þǣra daga, ġif man ǣniġe ǣddran ġe-openað on þǣre tīde, þæt hit bið his līf-lēast, oððe langsum sār. Þæs cunnode sum lǣċe, lēt his horse blōd on þǣre tīde, and hit lǣġ sōna dēad.

The olden-time doctors (literally 'leeches') set-down in Latin-books, that on each month are always two days, that are very dangerous any drink/potion on to receive, or blood on (those days) to let. Because – one hour (literally 'tide') there-is on each of-those days, if one any vein opens on that hour, that it is his life-loss, or enduring disability (literally 'sore(ness)'). About-that experimented a-certain (literally 'some') doctor: he-let his horse's blood on that hour, and it lay/fell at-once (literally 'soon') dead.

From The Herbals

Based on Latin and ultimately Greek originals, the OE Herbals were valiant efforts to record ancient knowledge about the efficacy of herbal cures. The problem was then, as now, being certain of the exact species intended by the classical authors. Nonetheless, monastic gardens cultivated many herbs of practical use, and the rather sentimental names accorded some plants in AS times (hound's-tongue, fox's-glove, hen-bell, etc.) may have been valid learning aids for novices.

Wælwyrt

Wið næddran slite ġenim þās ylcan wyrte þe we 'ebulum' nemdun, ǣr þām ðe þu hy forċeorfe heald hy on þīnre handa & cweð þrīwa nigon sīþan: 'omnes malas bestias canto' þāt ys þonne on ūre ġeþēode 'Besing & ofercum ealle yfele wild-dēor'...

Walwort – Against adder's bite, take this plant, which we 'ebulum' named, (and) before you it ust, hold it in your hand and say thrice nine times: 'Omnes malas bestias canto', that is, in our tongue: 'Enchant and vanquish all evil beasts.'

Pionia

Ðēos wyrt ðe man 'peonian' nemneð wæs funden fram Peonio þām ealdre & hēo þone naman of him hæfð. Hēo bið ċenned fyrmest in Grecam þā ēac se mǣra ealdor Homerus on hys bōcum amearcode. Hēo bið funden swȳþost fram hyrdum & hēo hæfð corn þǣre myċelnesse þe *maligranati* & hēo on nihte scīneð swā lēoht-fæt &...hēo byð, swā we ǣr cwǣdon, oftust fram hyrdum on nihte ġemēt & ġegaderod.

Peony – This plant that people call Peonia was found/identified by Peonius the scholar and she/it the name from him takes. She is born/found-growing originally in Greece where also the famous scholar Homer in his books mentioned (her). She is found mostly by shepherds and she produces pods of-the size that (has) (a) pomegranate and she at night glows like (a) lighted lamp, and... she is, as we before said, most-often by shepherds at night met-with and gathered.

Bee Charm

Once a year, bees irritate their 'owners' by relocating ('swarming'). Controlling this process is tricky, and a charm was developed to assist. It may be viewed as white magic to combat dark forces. In the second verse, the bees are addressed as *sige-wif* ('women of victory' or 'war-wives'), bringing to mind the word 'Valkyrie' (in OE wælcȳrie or 'choser of the slain') – a term of flattery if not of approval?

Wið ymbe nim eorþan, ofer-weorp mid þīnre swīþran handa under þīnum swīþran fēt,

Against bees (Swarming), take earth, throw (it) with your stronger (i.e. right) hand under your right foot

and cwet:

and say:

Fō iċ under fōt, funde iċ hit.

Put I (it) under foot, found/settled I it

Hwæt, eorðe mæġ wið ealra wihta ġehwilċe

Lo! Earth/soil can (work) against of-all (evil) beings each

and wið andan and wið ǣminde

and against malice and against malice

and wið þā miċelan mannes tungan.

and against the powerful person's tongue.

And wiððon forweorp ofer grēot, þonne hī swirman, and cweð:

And then throw over (them) grit/soil, when they swarm, and say:

Sitte ġē, sīġe-wīf, sīgað tō eorþan!

Settle ye, war-wives, sink to (the) earth!

Nǣfre ġēwilde tō wuda flēogan.

Never you wild to woodland should-fly.

Bēo ġē swā ġemindiġe mīnes gōdes,

Be you as mindful of-my good/benefit,

swā bið manna ġehwilċ mētes and eþeles.

As is of-men each of-meat/food and home.

Dictionary of Old English

NOTE

The dictionary section is designed to help you cope with a range of words typical of the easier and more popular OE texts, in the forms you are likely to meet them in.

As well of being of general application, the dictionary covers a specially designed selection of texts that takes you beyond the short examples included in this new edition. The texts themselves can be accessed on the internet at **www.indigogroup.co.uk/oereader/**, and comprise a collection of excerpts from OE prose and verse, arranged by subject. They are designed both to help you with reading practice and give you a sense of how the Anglo-Saxons regarded the world around them – from a very different set of ideas and level of knowledge from that we take for granted!

SCOPE AND AIM

This dictionary contains some three-and-a-half-thousand of the commonest words in Old English (Anglo-Saxon) and should be useful to beginners in translating simple passages of Old English prose and verse from any source, as well as to more advanced students as a rapid reference aid. The *User Friendly Dictionary* lists words by order of the consonants they contain, rather than by the usual strict alphabetical order of all letters in the word. The variation in Old English (OE) in stressed vowels at different times and in different dialects, plus many variants of spellings, make conventional OE dictionaries awkward to look words up in – you are constantly referred to another entry. This problem is largely eliminated here, and after even a little practice, the user should find this dictionary offers an easy and speedy way to locate the right OE word.

ORDER OF WORDS

Words are listed by order of their consonants; vowels are only taken into account in ordering words within an identical consonant profile. Inflected endings are generally ignored in establishing the order e.g. the final *-eð* or *-ede* of a verb or *-um* or *-an* of a noun will not be taken into account except in cases like *dōð* where it can hardly be avoided. Similarly prefixes e.g. *ā-*, *on-*, *be-*, *ġe-* are usually ignored in listing words, though quite a few common examples will also be found listed under their prefixed forms. Such prefixes are usually unstressed in pronunciation. Compounds (word-combinations) are not listed as such unless particularly common or with a specialised meaning; otherwise, these should be looked up under their constituent elements which is arguably the best way of understanding how the compound is built anyway.

Summary:
       look for *ġelysted* and *lāst* under L*S
       look for *wiðcweðan* under W*TH or CW*
look for *mānscaða* under M*N and SC* and combine the meanings of the two elements.

*

ā/ō	adv. 'ever, always'
ā-	(?a-) unaccented verb prefix
ǣ	F. 'law, 'religion'
ǣ	'water'-; 'religion-'
ēa	'river' *obl.* īe
ī	= ġe-

*B

ebba	m. 'ebb-tide'
abbod	M. 'abbot'
abbodisse	f. 'abbess'
ebrisc	adj. 'Hebrew'
āc	M. 'oak (tree)'
ac	conj. 'but; and'
ēċe	adj. 'eternal'
ēac	adv. 'also'
ēaca	m. 'increase'
iċ	pron. 'I'
īeċ-eð	'increases, augments' *p.* ȳcte
ecg	F. 'edge, point; sword'; as pref. 'sword-'
acol	adj. 'dismayed, scared'
ēcum/ēcan	*obl.* of ēċe 'eternal'
ā-cenð	I 'gives birth to'
ēacn-að	II 'increases, is enlarged'
ācennednes	F. 'birth'
ēacnung	F. 'increase'
ēcnes	F. 'eternity'
æcer	M. 'field, acre' *pl.* acras
ȳcte	*p.* 'increased'

*D

ād	'funeral pyre'
ed-	'again'
ēode	*p.* 'went' *pl.* ēodon
ēad	N. 'riches, good fortune'
ēad-	= ēad- 'rich' or eað- 'easy, humble'
ēadiġ	adj. 'blessed, prosperous, lucky'
ādl	FN 'disease'
īd(e)l	adj. 'worthless, vain, empty'
edlēan	N. 'reward, recompense'
adūne	adv. 'below; down'
ēaden	*pp.* 'granted, decreed'

oden	F. 'threshing-floor'
ed-nīwe	adj. 'new, renewed'
ǣdre	adv. 'speedily; entirely'
ǣdre/ēdre	f. 'artery'
ādrinċ-eð	'drowns, perishes'
īdes	F. 'lady'
ādiligode	*p.* 'destroyed'
edsceaft	F. 'new being, renewal'
edwist	F. 'food, substance'
edwīt	N. 'reproach, abuse'

*F

of	prep.+*dat.* 'from, out of'; adv. 'away, off'
of-	'off-, out-' (intensive/destructive)
ofbeat-an	'to beat to death'
of-ēode	*p.* 'he obtained, extorted'
of-dæle	N. 'slope, chasm'
of-dōn	'to remove'
of-dūne	adv. 'down'
ofġief-eð	'gives up, quits'
of-gān	'to obtain, extort'
of-hende	adj. 'absent'
yfel	adj. 'evil' *gen.* yfles
yfle	adv. 'evilly, wrongly'
of-feall-an	'to fall on, kill; to fall away'
of-leġd	*pp.* 'laid down'
of-let	*p.* 'gave up'
of-man	*p.* 'forgot'
yfemest	adj. 'upmost'
ǣfen	M. 'evening' *gen.* ǣfnes
æfn-að	'performs, achieves', *p.* æfnade
efen	adj/adv 'even, equal'
efn-	'just-as, equally'
efne	adv. 'even, quite, likewise'
ofen	M. 'furnace, oven' *gen.* ofnes
ufan	adv. 'from above, over'
ǣfnung	F. 'evening'
efen-līca	m. 'equal, like'
efen-lǣċe	I 'imitates'
ufan-weardum	adv. 'above'
ā-fȳr	'drive away!'
ā-fēar-ed	*pp.* 'frightened'
ǣfre	adv. 'ever, always'

57

[*F]
eofor M. '(wild) boar, boar-helm'
eafora m. 'son, heir'
ōfer M. 'edge, bank, shore' gen. ōfres
ofer prep. 'beyond, over, across'
adv. 'over, across; in excess'
ofer- 'across, over; excessive'
offr-að 'offers, sacrifices' p. offrade
ufor adv. 'higher'
oferbrǣd-an 'to spread over, overshadow'
ofer-hȳrnes F. 'transgression, omission'
ofer-hygd FN 'pride, arrogance'
ofer-mōd adj. 'proud'; subst. 'pride, overconfidence'
ofer-mǣte adj. 'excessive'
ofer-mētto F.pl. 'pride'
offrung F. 'offering'
ofer-sēon 'to survey; look down on; reject'
ofer-swīðan I 'to overpower'
ofer-wrēon 'to cover, conceal' pp. oferwriġen
of-scēoteð 'shoots down'
of-slēan 'to cut off, strike down, destroy' p. ofslōg, pp. ofsleġen
of-snīð-an 'to cut off, kill'
ǣfæst adj. 'pious'
efst 'hastens'
ofost F. 'haste'
ǣ-fæstnes F. 'religion'
oft adv. 'often' sup. oftost
ofett N. 'fruit, vegetable'
of-tēah p. 'withheld'
æfter prep.+dat. 'after, according to, through'
æfterra adj. 'following, next'
of-ðynċeð 'it displeases, vexes s.one'
ufeweard adj. 'upward'

*G
ǣġ N. 'egg' pl. ǣgru
ǣġ pref. 'any-'
īġ F. 'island'
-iġ adjectival suffix
eġe M. 'awe, dread, fear'
ēaġe n. 'eye'
ǣġ-hwelċ pron. 'each'
ǣġ-hwǣr adv. 'anywhere'
ā-gol p. 'yelled out'
āglǣca m. 'monster, demon'
īġ-lond M. 'island'
agan 'to own'
ā-gān pp. 'gone' (gān)
āġen adj. 'one's own' gen. āgnes
ēgor M. 'flood, ocean'
eġesa m. 'monster, horror, fear'
eġesliċ adj. 'frightful'
ā-goten pp. 'overlaid'
ā-gǣð 'occurs' (gān)
ǣġðer pron. 'either, both'
iugoð F. 'age; youth'
ēaġe-ðyrel N. 'window'

*H
āh owns' (āgan)
ēoh M. 'yew-tree'
eoh MN 'war-horse' gen. ēos
ā-hebb-an 'to raise, lift up' pp. ā-hefen
āhte p. 'owned'
ǣht F. 'possession(s)'
ēht F. 'hostility, persecution'
ēht-eð I 'pursues, vexes'
eaht F. 'esteem, opinion'
eahta 'eight'
eaht-an 'to esteem, consider'; 'to pursue' p. eahtode
īhte p. 'increased'
ūht(e) Mf. 'half-light, pre-dawn'
ūht-sang M. 'Matins'
ǣġ-hwǣr adv. 'anywhere'
al- = eal 'all'
ele MN 'oil'
eall adj. 'all'
eal- 'very-, entirely-'

ēalā	'oh!, alas!'		ā-līes-an	I 'to release'
ealu	N. 'ale' *obl.* ealoð		eallswā	adv. '(just) as; also; similarly'
ele-bēam	M. 'olive-tree'			
ǣlċ	adj./pron. 'each'		ealoð	*obl.* of ealu 'ale'
ōleċċ-eð	'flatters'		elðēode	*pl.* 'foreigners'
ōleċċung	F. 'flattery, something agreeable'		elðēodiġ	adj. 'foreign'
			ælwiht	M. 'monster'
ā-lecgan	I 'to lay down; abolish'			
elc-að	'tarries'		***M***	
elcung	F. 'delay'		ēam	'(maternal) uncle'
elcor	adv. 'elsewhere'		eom	I am
(for)ald-eð	'grows old'		ymb(e)	prep/adv. 'about, around; after'
eald	adj. 'old, ancient'			
eald-	'former, original, ancient'		ymb-	ċierr-an 'to revolve'
ylde	M.*pl.* 'men'		ymb-gang	M. 'circuit'
yldo	F. 'age, period; old age'		ymb-hȳdiġ	adj. 'anxious'
yld-an	'to delay'		ymb-hoga	m. 'a care, worry'
yldra	adj. 'older, elder'		ymb-hwyrft	M. 'orbit, revolution'
vldran	*pl.* 'ancestors'			
ealdor	N. 'life'		umbor	N. 'infant'
ealdor	M. 'elder, master' *gen.* ealdres		ymb-sittan	'to surround, besiege'
ealdor-dom	M. 'lordship'		ymb-ūtan	prep/adv. 'around, about'
ealdor-mann	M. 'earl, shire-officer'		ōmiġ	adj. 'rusty'
			imp-ian	'to graft'
olfend(a)	Mm 'camel'; or = ylpend 'elephant'		ǣmette	f. 'ant'
			ǣmetta	m. 'Leisure
ylfete	F. 'swan'			
ealg-að	'defends'		***N***	
ealh	'temple' *gen.* ēales		ān	adj./pron. 'one, a'
eolh	M. 'elk'		ann/onn	'grants' *pl.* unnon
eolh-secg	M. 'papyrus, reed'		ǣnne	*acc.* of ān ('one')
æl-mihtiġ	adj. 'almighty'		in	prep. 'in. into, on' etc
ælmessan	*pl.* 'almsgiving, charity'		in	adv. 'on, in'
ellen	N. 'zeal, valour'		inn	N. 'lodging'
ellen-	'powerful-, heroic-'		inne	adv. 'inside'
elne	adv. 'zealously, keenly'		on	= in
elniend	adj. 'zesty, increasing in strength'		on-	'in-, into-, on-' (but often redundant); 'un-'
ellende	adj. 'foreign'		ono	'lo!'
ealneġ	adv. 'always'		unbindan	'to untie'
ēa-lond	N. 'island'		onbryrd	*pp.* 'excited; incited'
eallunga	adv. 'entirely'		onbīt-an	prep./adv. '(a)round, about'
ylp/elpend	M. 'elephant'			
ellor	adv. 'elsewhere'; adj. 'other'		inċ	*acc,dat.* 'you two'
			unc	*acc,dat.* 'us two'
ealles	adv. 'entirely'		incofa	m. 'inner room; heart'
elles	adv. 'otherwise, besides'		unclǣne	adj. 'unclean, impure'
eles	*gen.* of ele 'oil'			

[*N]
oncnaweð 'knows, perceives' *p.* oncnēow
ancora m. 'hermit'
ancor M. 'anchor'
inċer 'belonging to both of you'
uncer 'belonging to us both'
unċyst F. 'vice, fault'
uncūð adj. 'unknown, strange'
oncweðeð/oncwyð 'answers; echoes'
and conj. 'and'
ānæd 'desert, wasteland'
ende M. 'end'
ġe-end-aðII 'ends'
endebyrd(nes) F. 'order, orderliness; development'
ende-dæġ 'day of death'
ondġiet/andġyt N. 'understanding, meaning'
ondleofen F. 'food'
endlyfta 'eleventh'
andlēan N. 'requital'
endemes adv. 'entirely; together'
ondōn/undōn, ondēð 'to undo; cancel'
under prep. 'under. beneath, below'
under-fōn 'to accept, undertake'
under-ġieteð 'perceives'
undern M. 'morning'
undyrne adj. 'unsecret, public'
understond-eð 'understands'
ondrǣt 'fears' (ondrǣdan)
andett-an I 'to acknowledge, confess'
andswar-ian II 'to answer, reply' *p.* andswarede
andswaru F. 'an answer'
andwlita m. 'face, countenance'
andweard adj. 'present, current'
andwyrdan I 'to answer
ān-floga m. 'solitary flier'
onfōn, onfēhð 'to take, accept' *p.* onfēng
onufon prep.+*dat.* 'above, upon'
unforcūð adj. 'honourable'
unfrið M. 'breach of the peace'

ǣniġ adj./pron. 'any'
enge adj. 'narrow, restricted, painful'
uniġ- = unġe-
inġehygd F. 'conscience, thoughts'
engel M. 'angel' *pl.* englas
unġeliċ adj. 'unalike'
Engle M.*pl.* 'Anglians, English'
Angel-cyn N. 'the English'
Engla-lond 'England'
englisc adj. 'English, Anglo-Saxon'
onġyld-an 'to pay, make up for'
onġemong prep.+*dat.* 'among, during'
unġemete adj./adv. 'immense(ly)'
onġēan prep./adv. 'opposite, over-, against'
anġinn N. 'beginning'
onġinneð 'begins, sets about' *p.* ongann
ingang M. 'entry, access'
onġēan-weard 'back to'
onġyred *pp.* 'unfastened'
unġerād adj. 'ignorant, wrong'
onġit-eð 'understands, realises' *p.* onġeat, onġēaton
unġewiss adj. 'inexperienced'
unhold adj. 'disloyal'
unhiere adj. 'horrible, wild'
ān-liċ adj. 'special, beautiful'
anlȳcnes F. 'similar thing; statue'
onǣled *pp.* 'enkindled'
onlāh *p.* 'loaned'
ān-līpe adj. 'single, individual'
unlȳtel adj. 'quite large'
onlūt-an 'to bow, bend'
onmiddan prep.+*dat.* 'amidst'
ān-mōd adj. 'resolute, single-minded'
onemn prep.+*dat.* 'alongside, near'
innan prep./adv. 'within, from within'
oninnan +*dat.* 'inside'
ġe-unnen *pp.* 'granted'
ānunga adv. 'straight away; entirely'

onuppan prep.+*dat*. 'upon';
 adv.'additionally'
ān-rǣd adj. 'resolute'
unrǣd M. 'folly'
unriht adj./subst. 'wrong'
unriht-hǣmed N. 'adultery'
unrīm N. 'a countless number'
onrǣs M. 'onrush'
unrōt adj. 'sad'
onsǣġednes F. 'sacrifice, offering'
ansīen F. 'visage, face, appearance'
ansund adj. 'sound, healthy'
onsend-an I 'to send, forward'
onspon *p*. unfastened, revealed'
onsæt *p*. 'occupied; menaced'
onsteal M. 'a supply'
onstell-anI 'to ambush'
instæpes adv. 'directly'
onstyred *pp*. 'agitated'
ent M. 'giant'
onett-eð I 'hastens'
unnyt adj. 'useless'
antimber 'material, substance'
ontȳned *pp*. 'opened'
intinga m. 'subject, reason'
untrum adj. 'infirm, ill'
untwēoġendliċ adj. 'certain'
innoð MF. 'insides, womb'
unēaðe adj. 'difficult, hard'
unǣðele adj. 'ignoble, common'
unþonc M. 'ingratitude, disservice'
unþēaw M. 'vice, sin'
onweġ adv. 'away'
onweald/anwald M. 'authority, power'
unwillum adv. 'reluctantly'
unwealt adj. 'unstable'
inweard adj. 'inner'
unwearnum adv. 'unstoppably'
unweorð adj. 'worthless'
inwit N. 'malice, wickedness'

*P
ūp/upp adv. 'up'
uppe adv. 'above'

ypp-eð 'opens. discloses, reveals'
 pp. ypped
ūp-ahebban 'to lift or raise up'
æppl M. 'apple' *pl*. applas
ūplond N. 'country, rural area'
open adj. 'open, evident, clear'
uppon adv. 'from above, upon'
open-liċ adj. 'plain, public'
apostol M. 'apostle'
epistola m. 'letter'
ūpweard(es) adv. 'upwards'

*R
ār M. 'messenger'; 'honour, mercy'; 'oar'; N. 'copper'
ār-að II 'honours, spares'
ǣ adv./prep. 'before, already'
ēar 'ocean'; 'earth'
ēare n. 'ear'
er-að 'plows' *p*. erede
or- 'without'; 'ancient'
ōr N. 'beginning, start'
ōra m. 'border, edge'; 'ore'
ūr M. 'aurochs, bison'
ūre adj. 'our'
yrre 'anger, wrath' *gen*. yrres; adj. 'angry'
ark/earc Ff. 'chest; ark'
orc M. 'ghoul'; 'cup'
ærċe-biscop M. 'archbishop'
eorcnan-stān M. 'precious stone'
or-cnǣweadj. 'well-known'
orċeard M. 'orchard'
ārod adj. 'honoured'
arod adj. 'prompt, quick'
eard M. 'native land, home, place'
eard-að 'inhabits' *p*. eardode
-eardiend '-dweller'
eardung F. 'abode'
ēored NF. 'mounted troop'
ord M. 'point (e.g. of origin)'; 'front-rank; source'
ord-fruma m. 'start, origin'
orf N. 'cattle' etc.
yrfe N. 'inheritance, heritage'
aræfn-an 'to perform'

[*R]

earfoðe	N.	'hardship, trouble'; adj. 'difficult, hard'
earfoð-		'difficult-to, hard-to'
eriġean		'to plow' *p.* erede
earg/earh	adj.	'cowardly, rotten'
earh	F.	'arrow'
eorl	M.	'(brave) man; earl'
eorl-liċ	adj.	'manly'
orlēġe	adj.	'hostile'; N. 'contention'
ār-lēas	adj.	'impious'
earm	M.	'arm'
earm	adj.	'wretched, vile'
ormōd	adj.	'hopeless, in despair'
yrmde	*p.*	'harassed'
eormen-		'powerful-, huge-'
yrming	M.	'wretch'
ormǣte	adj.	'huge, immoderate'
yrmð(u)	F.	'misery'
arn	*p.*	'ran'
ærn	N.	'hall; room'
earon		'are'
earn	M.	'eagle'
īren	N.	'iron'
iernan, irn-ð		'runs' p. arn, urnon
ǣrende	M.	'message, errand'
yringa	adv.	'in anger'
ġe-earnung		'merit, desert'
eornoste	adj.	'earnest, serious'
orped	adj.	'decisive, active'
ǣrest	adj.	'first, earliest'
ǣrist		'resurrection'
orsorg	adj.	'unconcerned, carefree'
eart		'are'
ōret	M.	'fight'
ōretta	m.	'warrior'
ortrȳwe	adj.	'hopeless; faithless'
eorðe	f.	'earth, soil, world' obl. *eorðan*
eorð-	'of this world'	
oroð	N.	'breath(ing)'
yrð	F.	'plowing; crop'
eorðliċ	adj.	'earthly'
yrð-ling	M.	'ploughman'
orðanc	N.	'intelligence, cleverness'
orðung	F.	'breath'
ǣr-ðan-ðe	conj.	'before'
orwēna	adj.+*gen.*	'in despair (of)'

*S

assa	m.	ass
ǣs	N.	'food'
īs	N.	'ice'
is/ys		'is'
ūs	*acc,dat.*	'us'
æsc		'ash (tree); object made of ash, boat, spear'
ascian/askian		'to ask' *p.* ascode
ġe-ascian II		'to hear of, learn of'
yslan	*pl.*	'embers'
esne	M.	'common man, servant'
īsen	N.	'iron'
ūsser		'our'
īsern	N.	'iron'
ēst	F.	'favour, approval'
ēast	adv.	'east(wards)'
ȳst	F.	'storm, tempest'
āstīhð		'climbs' *p.* āstāh (stīgan)
ēastan	adv.	'easterly, from the east'
ostre	f.	'oyster'
Eastron	f.*pl.*	'Easter'
Eastseaxe*pl.*		'East Saxons, Essex'
ēast(e)weard		'eastwards'

*T

ǣt		'food'
æt	prep.	'at, by, from'
it-eð, itt, eteð		'eats (up)'
ūt	adv.	'out'
ūt-āberstan		'to break out'; sim. ūtberstan
ūt-ādōn		'to put out'
ūt-drīfeð		'drives away'
ætforan	prep.	'in front of, before'
ætgædere	adv.	'together'
ætgifa	m.	'food provider'
ūt-gang	M.	'exit'
atol	adj.	'awful, fearful'
ūtemest	adj.	'ultimate, uttermost'
eoten	M.	'giant'
ūtan	adv.	'(from) outside'
ūtanweard		'outside'
ātor	N.	'poison' *gen.* āttres

ūter(r)a adj. 'outer'
ǣtren adj. 'poisonous'
ætīewde/ætēowde *p.* 'displayed'
ætȳwð I 'shows'
ūteweard adj. 'external'

*TH
āð *pl.*-as 'oath'
ēaðe/ēðe adj. 'easy'; adv. 'easily'
ēð-/ēað-/ȳð- 'easy-to'
ēð-an 'to breathe' *p.* ēðedon
īeð adv. 'more easily'
oð prep. 'up to, as far as, until'; conj. 'until'
oð- 'apart-, away-'
oððe conj. 'or'; 'either...or'
ūðe *pl.* ūðon 'granted'
ȳð F. 'wave; water'
ȳð-beġeata adj. 'easily obtained'
oð-beor-eð 'bears away'
oð-feall-eð 'fails; declines'
æðele adj. 'noble'
ēðel NM 'own land or home' *gen.* ēðles
ēaðe-lic adj. 'simple, unimportant'
āðeling M. 'princeling, noble'
ēaðmettu F. 'humility'
ēað-mōd adj. 'gentle, kind'
āðen-ian 'to stretch, draw out'
ōðer adj./pron. 'other, another, the second; some ... some' *gen.* ōðres
āuðer pron. 'someone, anyone/thing'; conj. 'either... or...'
oþþæt conj. 'until'
oð-īew-an 'to demonstrate; appear' *p.* oðīewde
ūð-wita m. 'scholar, philosopher'

*W
āwa adv. 'for ever'
ēow *acc.,dat.* 'you, to you'
āweċċ-an 'to awake, make rise' *p.* āwehte
ēawde/ēwed FN. 'flock of sheep'
ġe-ȳwed *pp.* 'shown'

aweġ adv. 'away'
āwiht adv. 'at all'; subst. 'anything'
āwerġed *pp.* 'accursed'
ēower adj. 'your'

*X
ax-ian 'to ask' *p.* axode
eax/æcs F. 'axe' *pl.* axe
eax/ex F. 'axle, axis'
oxa m. ox
eaxl F. 'shoulder'
axan *pl.* 'ashes'

B*
bā adj. 'both'
be/bī +*dat.* 'by, about, along'
be- pref. makes vb. trans. etc.
bēo 'be!'
bēo f. 'bee'

B*B
bebod N. 'command'

B*C
bæċ N. 'back'; *pl.* bacu; under-bæċ 'behind'
bēċe F. 'beech'
bōc F. 'book' *pl.* bēċ
bucca m. 'goat'
bæċ-bord N. 'port (side)'
bycgan I 'to buy'
bōc-land N. 'land by title, alienable land'
becum-að 'arrives, meets, happens' *p.* becōm
bēacn N. 'sign, banner, symbol'
bīecn-að 'signals, signifies'
bæcere M. 'baker'
bōcere M. 'scholar'
bōc-cræft M. 'learning'

B*D
bād *p.* 'awaited' (bīdan)
bǣd-eð 'urges, requires'
bæd, bǣdon *p.* 'asked' (bidan)
ġebed N. 'prayer' *pl.* ġebedu
bedd N. 'couch'
ġebedda m. 'bedfellow, mate'

[B*D]
bēad   p. 'offered' (bēodan)
bēadu   F. 'war, battle' gen.
          beadwa/beaduwe
bēod   M. 'bowl, table'
bēod-eð/bīett 'offers,
          declares, orders' +dat.; p.
          bēad
bīd-eð   'waits' p. bād pp.
          ġebiden
gebīd-eð 'experiences'
bid-eð   'asks' p. bād, bǣdon
ġebid-eð 'prays' p. ġebidde
ġebod   N. 'command'
boda   m. 'messenger'
bōd-að   II 'preaches, declares' p.
          bōdade
būde, būdon 'dwelt'; 'bent'
bydel   M. 'messenger
bōdung   F. 'preaching'

B*F
bifian   II 'trembled, shuddered'
          p. bifode
bufan   prep. 'above'
beforan   +dat. 'before, ahead of'
beæftan   +dat. 'behind'

B*G
bēag/bēg M. 'ring, arm-ring'
bēag   p. 'bent' (būgan)
bēġ-ð   = būgeð 'bends'
be-gāð   'does, serves' etc (begān)
biġ-   = 'be', 'by' etc
bīeġ-eð   'turns; makes bend' p.
          biġde/bēġde
bēġde   p. 'turned' (bīegan)
be-gān   'to cross: inhabit, attend
          to, cultivate; pratice,
          worship'
bēġen   adj. 'both'
beginn-eð 'to begin' p. began
beġeondan   prep. 'beyond'
bīgeng   F. 'observance, habit'
bīgong   M. 'circuit. region'
bōg   M. 'bough'; 'arm'
boga   m. bow'
bēgra   'of both'

beġīeteð 'obtains; begets'
būg-eð   'bends, bows' p. bēag
bȳg-eð   'dwells'

B*H
bēah   = bēag 'ring'
bōh   = bōg 'bough; arm'
behōf-að 'it behoves, is necessary'
behēafdod   pp. 'beheaded'
beheald-eð   'gazes on, preserves
beheon-an   +dat. 'on this side of
bōhte   p. 'bought'
behāteð   'promises'

B*L
bǣl   N. 'fire, bonfire'
belle   m. 'bell'
bealu   F. 'harm, injury, evil' pl.
          bealwa; adj. 'harmful,
          evil'
bealo-   'wicked, harmful'
bill   M. 'sword, chopper'
bolla   m. 'bowl'
bealċ-eð 'belches (out)'
bælċ   M. 'pride'
belūċ-eð 'shuts up, locks in'
bulluc   M. 'bullock'
bold   N. 'house, hall'
beald/bald   adj. 'bold'
bield-eð 'exhorts; builds'
ġebyld   pp. 'emboldened'
byldo/bieldu F. 'boldness,
          arrogance'
bald-līċe adv. 'boldly'
baldor   M. 'lord'
bīleofa   m. 'support, food'
beliġ-eð 'surrounds' (belicgan)
ġe-belg   M. 'anger'
ġe-bolgen pp. 'swolen with emotion;
          angered, enraged'
belhð   'angers' (belgan)
belimp-eð   'belongs; happens'
          p. belamp
bolster   MN. 'cushion, pillow'
          gen. bolstres
belīð   'surrounds' (belicgan)
bile-wit adj. 'pure-minded'
bealwa   pl. of bealu 'harm'

64

BL*

blēo	N.	'hue, colour, show'
		gen. blēos *dat.pl.* bleowum
blāc	adj.	'pale, shiny'
blæċ	adj.	'black'
blīċ-eð		'shines'
blæċ-ern	N.	'lantern'
blǣd	M.	'success, fame'; 'breath, blast'
blēd	F.	'fruit, crop'
bledu	F.	'bowl'
blōd	M.	'blood'
blōma	m.	'nugget
blend-eð		'blinds'
blinn-eð		'ceases, tails off'
blind	adj.	'blind'
ġeblond	N.	'swirl'
ġeblonden	*pp.*	'mixed, blended'
blonden-feax	adj.	'grizzle-haired'
bliss	F.	joy'
blissode	+*gen.*	'rejoiced (in)' (blissian)
blast	M.	'blast (of wind, fire)'
blōstma	m.	'flower
blāt	adj.	'ghastly, livid'
blōt	N.	'sacrfice'
blēts-ian		'to bless' *p.* blētsode
blētsung	F.	'blessing'
blīðe	adj.	'happy': sim. blīþ-ful
blāw-eð		'blows' *p.* blēow
blōw-eð		'blooms' *p.* blēow *pp.* blōwen

B*M

bām/bǣm *dat.*		'to both'
bēam	M.	'tree, beam'
bēom		'I am'
bīeme	f.	'trumpet'

B*N

bān	N.	'bone'
bana	m.	'killer'
bann-an		'to summon'
ġebann	N.	'summons, ordinance'
bēn	F.	'petition'
benn	F.	'wound'
bēan	F.	'bean, pea'
bēon		'to be'
inn	F.	'container, manger'
bū-an		'to dwell'
būne	f.	'beaker'
benċ	F.	'bench'
bān-cofa	m.	'bone-box, body'
bend		'bond, chain'
bindeð/bint		'binds' *p.* band *pp.* ġebunden
bōnda	m.	'freeman, commoner'
-būende		'-dwellers'
bān-hring	M.	'vertebra'
benām	*p.* +*gen.*,*dat.*	'deprived (of)' (beniman)
bint		'binds' (bindan)
binnan		+*dat..* 'within, inside'
beneoðan +*dat.*		'beneath'

B*R

bār	M.	'boar'
bar-um etc.		*obl.* of bǣr 'bare'
gebǣre	N.	'bearing, behaviour; outcry
-bǣre		(suff.) '-carrying'
bǣr	adj.	'bare' *obl.* bar-
ber-að		'bares' *p.* berode
ber-eð		'bears' *pp.* ġeboren 'born'
bera	m.	'bear'
bere	M.	'barley'
bearu	M.	'grove of trees' *gen.* bearwes
bēor	N.	'beer'
gebēoras	M*pl.*	'drinking companions'
-bora		'-doer'
būr	N.	'room, chamber'
ġebūr	M.	'peasant-farmer'
ġebyr-að		'belongs, suits, happens' (ġebyrian)
beorc	F.	'birch-tree'
be-rād	*p.*	'overtook (on horseback)'
beard	M.	'beard'
bord	N.	'shield'; 'plank, deck'
borda	m.	'edge'
ġebyrd	F.	'birth, status'
beriġ	N.	'berry'
bearg	M.	'hog'

[B*R]
beorg M. 'hill'
ġebeorg N. 'protection, defence'
beorg-eð 'protects, saves' *pp.*
   ġeborgen
burg 'borough, walled town'
   dat. byriġ
ġebirg-eð 'tastes'
ġebyrged *pp.* 'buried'
be-byrgan I 'to bury'
byrgen F. 'burial, grave
burgware *pl.* 'citizens'
bearh *p.* 'protected'
burh = burg 'fortress' etc.
bierht-eð 'brightens, illuminates'
birhtu F. 'brightness'
beorht adj. 'bright, clear, fine'
bearhtm M. 'flash (of light, sound)'
byrele m. 'butler'
bearm M. 'bosom'
beorma m. 'yeast'
bearn N. 'child'
beorn M. 'man, soldier'
birn-eð/biern-eð 'burns' *p.* barn
ġeboren *pp.* 'born'
burne f. 'stream'
byren F. 'she-bear'
byrne f. 'chest-armour, mail-shirt'
berȳp-eð 'takes, strips' *p.* berȳpte
ġebēor-scipe M. 'company of drinkers'
berst-eð 'bursts, crashes' *p.* bærst
byrst 'great loss or damage

BR*
brū = brēaw 'brow'
brǣċ N. 'a breaking'
ġebrǣċ N. 'clash, noise'
breċ-eð/bricð 'breaks' *p.* brǣċ, brǣcon
brōc M. 'brook'
broc N. 'affliction, adversity, illness'
broc 'badger'
bruċ-eð 'uses, enjoys' +*gen*; *p.* brēac

brȳċe N. 'advantage, profit'; adj. 'useful'
bryce M. 'infringement'
brycg F. 'bridge'
ġebrocen *pp.* 'broken'
brād adj. 'wide, broad'
brǣd 'flesh'
brǣd-eð 'spreads' *p.* brǣdde
brǣd-eð 'draws, flexes, weaves' *p.* brūdon *pp.* brōden
bred F. 'plank; tablet'
brid M. 'chick'
brȳd F. 'bride'
brīdl M. 'rein'
brēg-að 'alarms, scares'
brego M. 'prince, chieftain'
brōga m. 'terror, danger'
breġd-eð 'draws, flexes; breeds' (= brēdeð); *ppl..* brugdon
briġd N. 'fluctuation of colour'
brōhte *p.* 'brought' (bringan)
breahtm M. 'loud noise'
brēme adj. 'famous'
brim N. 'sea'
brēm(b)el M. 'bramble'
brim-ðisa m. 'ship'
brūn adj. 'dark-and-glossy'
bryne M. 'a burning'
brand M. 'sword, torch, fire'
brenġeð/brinġeð I 'brings'
brant adj. 'deep, steep'
brerd M. 'rim, margin'
brord M. 'point, shaft'
bryrd-eð 'incites'
brosn-að II 'decays, rots'
brosnung F. 'decay'
brēost M. 'breast, heart'
brastl-að II 'crackles'
brēt/brītt = brēdeð 'flexes'
brytta m. distributor, giver'
bryttian II 'to divide up; to rule'
bryten- (pref.) 'spacious'
Bryt(en)lond N. 'Britain'
Bryttas/Brettas *pl.* 'Britons, Celts'
brēot-eð 'demolishes' *pp.*-broten
brǣð M. 'scent, vapour'
ā-brēoþan 'to decay, deteriorate'
brōðor M. 'brother' *dat.* brēþer

66

ġebrōþru M*pl* 'brothers, monks'
brēaw M. 'eye-brow, -lash'

B*S
basu adj. 'intense red' *obl.* basw-
bisceop M. 'bishop'
be-scēawað II 'scans'
bisgu F. 'preoccupation'
bysg-að 'is busy, troubles someone' *pp.* bysgad
beseah *p.* 'looked' (sēon)
bōsm M. 'bosom'
bismer M. 'insult, humiliation'
bismr-að 'insults, degrades'
bȳsen/bīsn F. 'example, model'
ġebȳsnung F. 'example'
besencte *p.* 'made sink, drowned'
bī-spell N. 'example. fable'
bist 'you are, will be'
besited 'besieges' *pp.* beseten
bestæl *p.* betook (themselves)

B*T
bāt FM 'boat'
bāt *p.* 'bit' (bītan)
bǣt-eð 'bridles'; 'worries at' *p.* ġebǣt *pp.* ġebǣted
ġebēt-eð *p.* ġebētte 'atones for, compensates'
bet adv. 'better'
bēat-eð 'beats' *ppl.* bēoton
bēot N. 'vow, boast, threat'
bīt/bīteð 'bites' *p.* bāt, biton
bīt = bīdeð 'asks'
bite M. 'bite, sting, cut'
bōt F. 'cure, remedy'
būtū pron. 'both'
betǣċeð 'entrusts'
bēotiġan 'to boast, pretend'
betǣhte *p.* 'entrusted'
botl = bold 'building, hall'
bytl-eð I, II 'builds'
betliċ adj. 'excellent'
bēotliċ adj. 'arrogant, aggressive'
botm M. 'bottom, foundation'

būtan +*dat.* 'except'; conj. 'unless, except
ġebiten *pp.* 'bitten'
betera adj. 'better'
bitter adj. 'harsh'
butere f. 'butter'
betst adv./adj. 'best, most'
betwēonum +*dat.* 'between'
betweox/betwix/betweoh +*dat.* 'between'; betwix þǣm þe 'while'

B*TH
bǣð N. 'bath' *pl.* baþu
bēoþ *pl.* 'are, will be'
biþ 'is, will be'
boþen rosemary

B*W
bȳw-eð 'polishes'
bewunden *pp.* 'surrounded'
bewriġen *pp.* 'covered'
bī-wist F. 'food'
bewitiġ-eð 'supervises'

C*
cū F. 'cow' *pl.* cȳ

C*C
ċēac 'jug'
ċēace f. 'cheek, jaw'
cuiċ/cwiċ adj. 'alive' *obl.* cucu
ā-cuc-iað 'they bring to life'
cycen N. 'chicken'
cȳdde *p.* 'declared, made known'

C*D
ġeċīd N. 'argument'
ċīdde *p.* 'chided; quarreled'
cudu 'cud'

C*F
cāf adj. 'active, energetic, bold'; sim. cāfliċ
cofa m. 'cupboard, cave'
ċeafl M. 'jaw/cheek(-bone)'

C*G
cǣġ　　　F. 'key'
ċīġ-eð　　'calls' *p.* ċiġde *pp.*
　　　　　ġeċieġed

C*H
ċehhetung　F. 'laughter,
　　　　　guffawing'

C*L
cēl-eð　　'cools'
ċēol　　　M. 'ship'
ċeole　　　F. 'throat'
ċiele　　　M. 'coolness'
cōl　　　　adj. 'cool'
cōl-ian　　II 'to grow cool'
cōl　　　　N. 'coal, burning matter'
cyll　　　F. 'leather bottle'
caliċ　　　M. 'chalice'
ċealc　　　M. 'chalk, lime'
ċeald　　　adj. 'cold'
ċild　　　N. 'child'
ċealf　　　'calf'
culfer　　*pl.* culfran 'dove'
cylen　　　'kiln, oven'
collen-ferhð　adj. 'proud,
　　　　　exultant'
columnan*pl.* 'pillars'

CL*
clēa　　= clawu 'claw'
clūd　　M. 'mass, lump
clif　　　N. 'cliff, rock'
clēof-eð　'cleaves, splits' *ppl..*
　　　　　clufon
tō-clīfst　'you split up'
clomm　M. 'fetter, chain, grip'
clymm-eð　　'climbs'
clǣne　　adj. 'pure, clean'
cling-eð　'adheres, shrinks' *p.*
　　　　　clang *pp.* clungen
clǣns-að　'cleans, purges'
clip-að　'calls out' *p.* cleopode
(be)clypp-eð　I 'embraces'
cleric-hādM. 'priesthood'
cluster　　'bar; cell'
clāð　　M. 'cloth; clothes'
clawu　　F. 'claw' *dat.pl.*
　　　　　clawum/clām

C*M
cum-eð/cymð 'comes, arrives' *p.*
　　　　　cīm(on), cwōm(on) *pp.*
　　　　　ġecymen
cuma　　m. 'new arrival, guest'
cyme　　M. 'arrival'
camp　　'battle, conflict'
cempa　　m. 'soldier, champion'
camp-stede　M. 'battlefield'
cumbol　N. 'standard, banner'
comēta　　'comet'

C*N
can　　'knows how to, can' *pl.*
　　　　cunnon
ċēn　　M. 'torch'
cēne　　adj. 'bold, brave'
ċen-eð　'gives birth to, creates' *p.*
　　　　ċenede
cunn-an　'to know how to'
cunn-ian, cunn-að 'tries, tests' *pp.*
　　　　ġecunnad
cyne-　　'royal-'
cyn　　N. 'kind, species, breed;
　　　　kin; people'
-cund　　'-like'
ġecynd　　F. 'own nature, type'
gecynde　adj. 'natural'
candel　　M. 'candle, lamp'
cynliċ　　adj. 'fitting'
cyneliċ　　adj. 'royal'
canon-bōc　M. 'church rule
　　　　book'
cyning　　M. 'king'
cynren　　N. 'kindred'
Cent　　'Kent'
Cantware *pl.* 'Kentish folk'
Cantwaraburg　F. Canterbury

CN*
ġecnucod *pp.* 'pounded, knocked'
cnapa　　m. 'youth, servant'
cnāw-eð　'knows' *p.* cnēow
cnēow　　F. 'knee'
cnearr　　M. 'small ship'
cnēoris　　F. 'generation: people'
cniht　　M. 'youth, servant'
cnōd-an　'to attribute to'

cnyss-eð 'tosses, crashes' *pp.*
ġecnysed/cnissed
cnōsl N. 'offspring'
cnotta m. 'knot'

C*P
cēp-eð 'seizes, guards, keeps, accepts'
ċēap M. 'cattle; any commodity'
ċīep-eð 'trades, buys, sells'
ġecōpliċ adj. 'correct, proper
cīepe-man M. 'merchant'
cypera *pl.* -n '(female) salmon'

C*R
caru F. 'care, concern
ċierr M. 'time, change'
ċier-eð 'turns, alters, converts' *p.* ċierde
cyre M. 'choice'
ċiriċe f. 'church'
carc-ern N. 'prison
ċeorf-eð 'carves, cuts down' *p.* ċearf, curfon *pp.* corfen
carful adj. 'anxious, diligent'
cariġ adj. 'anxious'
ċeorl M. 'churl, peasant, man, freeman'
ċirm M. 'outcry
curon *ppl.* 'chosen' *pp.* ġecoren
corn N. 'seed, tiny grain'
corðor F. 'troop' *pl.* corðre

CR*
crabba m. 'crab'
cræft M. 'strength, skill, art'
cræftiġ adj. 'powerful, cunning, learned'
cræft(i)gam. 'workman. craftsman'
crang *pl.* crungon 'fell, collapsed' (cringan)
crēop-eð 'creeps'
cristalla m. 'crystal'
crīsten adj. 'Christian'
crīstes mæl 'sign of the cross'
cræt N. 'waggon

C*S
ċēse 'cheese'
ċēos-eð 'chooses' *p.* ċēas, curon *pp.* ġecoren
cyss-eð I 'kisses'
ċeosel 'gravel, sand'
cosp M. 'fetter
cysp-eð 'fetters'
cāsere M. 'emperor'
ċist F. 'chest
ċīest/ċyst 'chooses' (ċēosan)
ċyst F. 'the best, an elite'
ċystiġ adj. 'virtuous, generous'
cost M. 'option, contingency'
cost-að II 'tempts'
castel M. 'castle, fortified town'
cost(n)ung F. 'temptation: affliction'
ċeaster F. 'city' *gen.* ċeastre
ċeaster-ware, -waran *pl.* 'citizens'

C*TH
cīð M. 'shoot, sprout'
coðu F. 'disease
cūð adj. 'well-known, familiar, evident'
cūðe 'knew (how to)' *pl.* cūþon
cȳðð F. 'homefolk, homeland'
cȳððeð/cȳðð 'declares, tells' *p.* cȳþde
cȳðere M. 'martyr

C*W
ċēow-eð 'chews'

CW*
cwiċ adj. 'living'
cweċ-eð 'shakes'
cwide M. 'saying, proverb etc'
cwedol adj. 'talkative'
cwiċ-seolfor N. 'mercury'
cwæde *pl.* cwædon 'said' *pp.* ġecweden (from cweðan)
cweht *pp.* 'shaken'
cwalu F. 'violent death'
cwel-eð 'kills' *ppl..* cwealdon
cwyld 'pestilence, destruction'

[CW*]
cwealm MN 'death, murder, plague'
cwielm-eð 'tortures, kills'
ġecwēme adj. 'agreeable'
cwēm-eð 'pleases'
cwōm p. 'came'
ā-cwan p. 'dwindled'
cwēn F. 'wife, woman, queen'
cwene f. 'woman, servant'
ā-cwenċan I 'to extinguish'
cweorn F. 'quern. handmill'
cweart-ern N. 'prison'
cwȳs-an I 'to crush, destroy'
cwið/cweðeð 'says, speaks'
cwæð p. 'said'

D*
dō 'do!' (dōn)

D*C
dīċ 'ditch, dike'
dīacon M. 'deacon

D*D
dǣd F. 'deed, act'
dēad adj. 'dead'
dyde 'did' etc. pl. dydon
dǣd-bōt F. 'penance, atonement
dēadliċ adj. 'perishable, mortal; deadly'

D*F
ġedēfe adj. 'fitting, suitable'
dēaf adj. 'deaf
dēaf p. 'dived'
dēofol M. 'devil' gen. dēofles
dēofol-ġield N. 'idolatory; idol'
ġedafen-að 'befits' +dat.
ġedafenliċ adj. 'fitting, proper'

D*G
dag-að 'it dawns'
dæġ M. 'day(time)' pl. dagas
dēag pl. dugon 'is good, useful, is worth' p. dohte
ġedīġ-eð 'endures, survives'
dæġ-hwāmliċ adj. 'daily'

dīgol adj. 'secret, hidden'
dīeglað 'hides, conceals'
dugon ppl.. 'availed'
dēagung F. 'dye'
dōgor M. 'day'.
dæġ-red N. 'daybreak'
dæġ-rīm N. 'a number of days'
duguð F. 'retinue, nobility; host; excellence'

D*H
dēah = dēag 'is good, useful, serves'
diht N. 'a dictate; disposition'
ġediht N. 'something written'
gediht-eð 'disposes; imposes; composes'
dohte 'served, was useful'
dohtor F. 'daughter' dat.sg. dehter

D*L
ġedāl N. 'sharing-out; a difference'
(tō)dǣl-eð I 'divides, shares out'
be-dǣl-eð 'deprives' +gen.
dǣl M. 'portion, part, area' pl. dǣlas
dæl N. 'valley' pl. dalu
dol adj. 'silly'
dolliċ adj. 'foolish, rash'
delf-eð 'digs' p. dealf
dolg/dolh MN. 'wound, scar'
dīl(e)gað 'obliterates' pp. (ā)dȳlegod

D*M
dēm-eð 'judges, decrees' p. dēmde
dēma m. 'judge'
demm M. 'injury, loss'
dimm adj. 'dim, gloomy'
dōm M. 'judgement. decree; glory'
-dom gen. -dōmes - abstract suffix

D*N

Dēne	M*pl.* 'the Danes'
denu	F. 'valley'
dōn, hē dēð	'do, put, cause, make' *p.* dyde
ġedōn	*pp.* 'done, accomplished'
dūn	F. 'hill'
of-dūne	*adv.* 'downwards'
dun(n)	*adj.* 'of a dingy colour'
dynede	*p.* 'boomed'
dincge	*m.* 'dung'
denisc	*adj.* 'Danish, Viking'
dynt	M. 'blow [or its effect]'

D*P

dēop	*adj.* 'deep, serious'
dēop-liċ	*adj.* 'profound'

D*R

daru	F. 'injury, damage' *gen.* dǣre
Dēre	M*pl.* 'the Deirans'
der-eð	'to damage, harm' *p.* derede
dear	*pl.* durron 'dares, presumes' *p.* dorste
dēor	N. 'wild animal; deer'
dēore	*adj.* 'dear, precious'
dor	N. 'door, passage'
duru	FN 'door' *pl.* dura/duru
dyrre	*subj.* 'might dare'
deorc	*adj.* 'dark, obscure, sinister'
ġedeorf	N. 'difficulty, danger'
dēorling	M. 'favourite'
durum	*dat.pl.* of duru 'door'
dēor-mōd	*adj.* 'courageous, worthy'
durron	*ppl..* 'they dare'
dyrne	*adj.* 'secret, problematical, wrong'
dorste	*p.* 'dared'
dyrstiġ	*adj.* 'adventurous'
daroð	F. 'javelin, spear'
dēor-wyrðliċ	*adj.* 'precious, splendid'

DR*

drȳ	M. 'sorcerer'
draca	*m.* dragon, serpent'
dreċ-eð	'troubles, disturbs'
drȳ-cræft	'magic'
ġedrēfed	*pp.* 'stirred up, agitated'
ġedrēfednes	F. 'tribulation'
drīfeð	'drives (out)' *p.* drāf
drag-an	'to drag, draw'
ġedræġ	N. 'throng'
drēog-eð	'works, lives, experiences' *p.* drēag *pl.* drugon
drȳġġe	*adj.* 'dry'
drȳġ-eð	'dries' *pp.* drūgod
(a)drīhð	= drēogeð
dryht	F. 'large crowd, people'
dryht-guma	*m.* 'warrior, retainer'
dryhten	M. 'ruler, lord, esp. God'
drihtnēum	*dat.pl.* 'corpses'
drihtscipe	M. 'bravery'
drohtað	M. 'way of life, context' *sim.* drohtnung
drēam	M. joy, ecstasy, music'
drȳman	I 'to sing aloud'
drenċ-eð	I 'supplies drink; drowns someone'
drinċ	M. 'drink'
drinċ-eð	'he drinks' *p.* dranc
ādrinċ-eð	'perishes by drowning'
ġedruncen	*pp.* 'drunk'
dreng	M. 'young warrior'
drep-eð	'strikes down'
drep	M. 'a blow, stroke'
drēop-eð	'drips'
dropa	*m.* 'a drop' *pl.* 'dew'
dryre	M. 'falling, cessation'
drēoriġ	*adj.* 'miserable; blood-stained'
drēorung	F. 'falling'
druron	*ppl..* see next word:
drēos-eð	'fails, perishes, gives out' *p.* drēas *pl.* druron
drūsade	*p.* 'drowsed'
drȳs	*gen.* of drȳ 'sorceror'
drysmað	II 'glowers'

D*S

disc	M. 'dish'
dysiġ	*adj.* 'foolish, stupid'
dysg-að	'commits errors'
dēst	'you do, make'

dūst N. 'dust'

D*TH
dēað M. 'death'
dēð 'he does, makes' *p.* dyde

D*W
dēaw 'dew'
dēawiġ adj. 'dewy'

DW*
dwel –eð *p.* dwelede 'leads or goes astray; deceives' sim. dwelað, dwolað
ġedwol adj. 'heretical'
ġedwola m. 'error, heresy'
dwolliċ adj. 'erroneous; heretical'
ġedwild N. 'error, heresy'
dweorg M. 'dwarf'
ġedwǣs adj. 'stupid, silly'
dwǣsc-eð 'extinguishes'

F*
fēa 'few'
(ġe)fēa M. 'joy'
fēo 'money' (= fēoh)

F*C
fæċ N. 'an interval of time' *gen.pl.* faca
feċċ-eð 'fetches, gets'
fāc(e)n N. 'deceit, treachery, crime' *pl.* fācnu
fǣcne adj. 'treacherous'

F*D
fad-að II 'supervises, arranges'
fēd-eð/fētt 'feeds' *p.* fēdde *pp.* ġefēd
fēode *p.* 'hated'
fōda m. 'food'
ġefadung F. 'organising'
fæder M. 'father'; eald— 'grandfather'
fōddor N. 'food, fodder'

F*F
fīf 'five'
fīfel N. 'large sea-monster'

fēf(e)r 'fever'
fīftiġ 'fifty'

F*G
fāg adj. 'spotted, speckled'
fāg = fāh 'inimical, stained'
fǣġe adj. 'doomed, fated'
ġefēġ N. 'joint'
fēġ-eð 'joins, unites'
fēog-eð 'hates'
fugol M. 'bird, fowl' *pl.* fuglas
fugoloð 'fowling'
fæġn-að II 'rejoices, is happy' +*gen.*
ġefæġen +*gen.* 'glad (at, of)'
fæġer adj. 'fair, lovely'
fæġre adv. 'prettily, kindly'

F*H
fāh adj. 'stained, tainted; hostile, criminal'
ġefeh/ġefeah 'rejoiced' *p.* ġefēgon
fēoh 'cattle, (movable) wealth' *gen.* fēos
fōh 'take!'
ġefeoht N. 'fight'
feoht-eð 'fights' *p.* feaht
fēhð F. 'hostility, feud'
fēhð 'he takes, holds, grabs' (fōn)

F*L
fela adj./subst.+*gen.* 'many'
fela- 'very-'
fell N. 'hide, skin-'
feall-eð 'falls; dies' *p.* fēoll
fealu adj. 'tawny, muddy-coloured' *gen.* fealwes
fēol-eð 'adheres to; penetrates; departs'
fola m. 'foal'
fūl adj. 'foul, impure'
full adj. 'full, complete'
ġefyll 'downfall, death, slaughter'
ġefyll-að I 'fulfill; fill'
fyll-eð I 'fells, destroys'
fyllo F. 'fulness'

folc	N. 'people, nation'	flot-mann	M. 'sailor'
folc-	pref. 'public-'	flōweð/flēwð	'flows' *p.* flēow
ġefylce	N. 'battalion'		
feld	M. 'open land, field'	**F*M**	
folde	f. 'earth'	fāmiġ	adj. 'foamy'
fold-	pref. 'earth-'	fæmne	f. 'maiden, woman'
fyldon	*ppl..* 'filled' *pp.* (ā)fyld	**F*N**	
folg-að	'follows, serves' *p.* folgode	fana	M. 'banner'
		fenn	'fen, marsh, moor'
folgoð	M. 'following, retinue'	fēon	'to hate'; 'to be glad'
fylg-eð	'pursues, follows, practices'	fēond	'enemy' *pl.* fȳnd
		ġe-fēonde	*p.* 'rejoiced'; adj. joyful'
fulluht	M. 'baptism'	fand-að	II 'tests, investigates'
folm	Fm. 'hand'	find-eð/fint	'finds, discovers' *p.* fond
ġefǣlsod *pp.* 'purged'			
fullǣst/fylst	M. 'help, support'	fund-að (tō)	'sets out for, strives for'
fvlst-eð	'helps' *p.* fylste		
fultum	M. 'help, aid'	(ġe)feng	M. 'grip, capture'
fultum-að	'helps, aids' *p.* fultumede	fēng	*p.* 'he took, grabbed'
fealw-að	'yellows, fades, ripens'	fengel	M. 'prince, lord'
fealwes etc.	*obl* of fealu 'tawny'	ġefangen *pp.* 'taken, caught'	
fȳlð	F. 'filth'	onfongen *pp.* 'received, admitted'	
fylð	= fealleð 'falls'	finger	M. 'finger'
fulwiht	'baptism'	fenix	M. 'phoenix'

FL*

flēa	'flea(s)'
flōc	'a flatfish'
flōd	M. 'flood; water'
flēog-eð	'flies' *ppl..* flugon
-floga	'-flier'
flēah	'flew'; 'fled'
flyht	M. 'flying, flight'
flīhð	'flees; puts to flight' (flēon)
flēam	M. 'flight (in battle)'
ġefliem-eð	'puts to flight'
flān	M. 'arrow'
flēon	'to flee; put to flight'
flōr	'floor, expanse, bed'
flȳs	N. 'fleece, coat'
flǣsc	N. 'flesh'
flett	N. 'floor; living-space'
ġe-flit	N. 'a contention, dispute; strife'
flēot-að	'floats' *p.* flēat, fluton
flot	N. 'sea'
flota	m. 'boat; fleet; sailor'
flot-here	M. 'pirate force'

FN*

fnǣst	M. 'a blowing, breathing'

F*R

fāra	*gen.pl.* 'of foes'
far-eð/færð	'goes' *p.* fōr(on) *pp.* ġefaren
fǣr	M. 'peril, sudden danger'
fǣr-	'sudden-, unexpected-'
fær	N. 'journey; locomotion' *pl.* faru
fēr-eð	'goes, departs' *p.* fērde
fer-að	'ferries, brings' *p.* ferode
ġe-fēra	m. 'comrade, companion'
fēara	*gen.pl.* 'of few'
feorr	adj. 'far (away)'
feor-að	'proceeds'
fīras	M*pl.* 'people, humans'
fīer-	'four-'
fōr	*p.* 'went' (faran)
ġefōr	*p.* died, passed on
fōr	F. 'expedition'
[F*R]	

for	prep. 'before, on account of'	for-lǣteð	'lets go, abandons; allows'
for-	prefix often denoting a destructive aspect	feorm	F. 'provision, feast; rent'
		feormað	'receives as a guest; sustains; consumes; polishes'
fore	prep. 'in the presence of; instead of'		
fore-	'beforehand; very'	forma	adj. 'first, earliest'
fȳr	N. 'fire'	fyrmest	'foremost, in the first place'
fyrr	adv. 'further'		
for-cūð	adj. 'evil, despised'	fearn	N. 'fern'
ā-fǣred/āfyrrde*pp*. 'frightened'		feorran	adv. 'from far back/off'; vb. 'to remove, distance'
fierd	F. '(general) army'		
fierd-wīte 'penalty for avoiding military service'		fērend	M. 'traveller'
		fīren	F. 'a crime'
fērde	*p.* 'went'	firen-	'wicked-, sinful-'
ford	M. 'ford'	foran	prep.+*dat.* 'before'
for-dēman	I 'to condemn'	foran tō	'beforehand'
for-dōn	'to destroy, corrupt'	fȳren	adj. 'fiery'
for-ġifan	'to grant, give over; forgive' *p.* forġeaf	fyrn-	'far-off, long-ago'
		fǣringa	adv. 'suddenly, unexpectedly'
for-ġieldan	'to pay up, indemnify'		
		for-nēah	adj. 'very near'
fore-ġīslas	M *pl.* 'hostages'	firen-lust	M. 'lustfulness'
fer-eð	= ferian 'to carry'	for-nam	*p.* 'deprived of, took away'
firgen-	'mountain-'		
for-ġeat	'forgot' *pl.* forġeāton	fēores	*gen.* of feorh 'life'
for-ġitolnes	F. 'forgetfulness'	feors-að	'proceeds: removes'
fearh	M. 'piglet' *gen.* fēares	fyrs	M. 'gorse-bush'
feorh	MN. 'life, soul' *gen.* fēores	fersc	adj. 'fresh'
		ġefēr-scipe	M. 'community, comradery'
for-habbað	'refrains, restrains from'		
		for-sēah	*p.* 'despised, renounced'
for-hāten *pp.* 'forsworn, false'		forst	M. 'frost'
ferhð	MN. 'mind, soul'	fyrst	adj. 'first'
ferhðloca m. 'body'		first	MN. 'a space of time'
for-hwī	'because'	fore-stihtung	F. 'predestination'
forht	adj. 'scared, timid'	fore-steall	'fine for robbery'
fyrhto	F. 'fright, dread'	for-sewen*pp.* despised'
forht-að	II 'is scared, dreads'	for-rotednes	F. 'corruption'
ferhtliċ	adj. 'just, honest'	faroð	M. 'shore'
for-hwega	adv. 'somewhat'	færð	'goes'
fǣrliċ	adj. 'sudden, unexpected'	ferð	= ferhð 'spirit'
ġefērlǣċ-eð	'associates'	fearðe	'fourth'
for-licgan 'to abandon'		forð	adv. 'forwards, onwards' etc; can = ferhð 'spirit, mind'
fǣreld	'journey, expedition'		
for-liġeð	'commits adultery'		
fyrlen	adj. 'remote'	forð-ian	'to accomplish, progress with'
for-liġer	M. 'adulterer'		

forðī 'because'
forð-fērde   p. 'passed on, died'
for-ðōht   pp. 'in despair'
for-ðǣm/for-ðon etc. conj./adv.
        'because, therefore'
furðum   adv. 'just as, quite,
        further'
ferðan   = furðum
forðenċeð'mistrusts'; cf. forðōht
furðor   adv. 'more distant'
furðrað   'furthers, promotes'
forð-sið   M. 'going forth, death'
fore-weard   adj. 'to the front,
        early'
for-wyrnan   'to prevent, to deny'
fyrwit   N. 'curiosity,
        inquisitiveness'

FR*
frēa   m. 'lord, esp. God'
frēo   adj. 'free'
freċ   adj. 'greedy, eager'
freca   m. 'champion'
frēċednes F. 'danger'
fricgan   'to ask'
frēcne   adj. 'dangerous, savage'
frēcennis 'danger
fracoð   adj. 'vile, contemptible'
ġe-frēdan 'to feel, sense'
frōd   adj. 'wise'
frēod   F. 'peace, goodwill'
frōfor   F. 'help, consolation'
frōfr-að   'gladdens, consoles'
frōfrend   'comforter e.g. the Holy
        Ghost'
ġefrǣġe   N. 'hearing, knowledge,
        report'
frīġe   pl. of adj. frēo 'free'
friġ-eð   'asks' (fricgan)
friġn-eð   'enquires'
frēoliċ   adj. 'free, free-born,
        generous'
frēols   'freedom, privilege;
        festival'
frēolsiað   'celebrate'
fram   prep.+*dat*. 'from, by,
        arising from'
from   adj. 'bold, energetic'
fruma   m. 'beginning, origin'

frum-   'first-'
frem-ian   II 'to benefit, help'
frem-eð   I 'does, commits' pp.
        ġefremed
fremde   adj. 'foreign, strange'
frum-sceaft   'origin, Creation,
        the original condition'
fremsumnes   F. 'kindness,
        generosity'
frum-stōl M. 'base, place of origin'
frymð   MF. 'start, origin'
frēan   gen. of frēa 'lord'
frīn-eð   'enquires' ppl.. frunon
ġe-frunen pp. 'learned, heard of'
franca   m. 'spear
Franc-land   'France'
frēond   M. 'friend' pl. frȳnd
frēond-rǣden   F. 'intimacy'
frēond-scipe   M. 'friendship'
frēoriġ   adj. 'icy'
fret-eð   'devours' p. frǣt
ġe-frǣtwade   pp. 'adorned'
frǣtwa   pl. 'treasures, ornaments'
frið   M. 'peace, sanctuary'
ġe-friðeð 'makes peace with,
        guards'

F*S
feos   gen.of fēoh 'cattle,
        wealth'
fūs   adj. 'eager'
fisc   M. 'fish'
fisc(n)að M. 'fishing'
fēa-sceaft adj. 'destitute'
fiscere   M. 'fisherman'
fæst   adj. 'secure, firm'
fæst-eð   'fasts'
fæstliċ   adj. 'firm, reliable'
fæsten   N. 'stronghold'; 'fasting'
ġe-fæstnode   p. 'fixed'
be-fæstan I 'to entrust, commit'
fōstor   M. 'sustenance, food'

F*T
fǣt   '(gold) plate'
fæt   N. 'vessel; bag' pl. fatu
fēt   'feeds'
fet-að   'to fetch' p. fetode
fētt   adj. 'fat'

[F*T]
fōt	M.	'foot' *pl.* fēt
fætels	M.	'vessel'
fetels	M.	'(sword-)belt'

F*TH
fēð		'he takes' (fōn)
fēða	m.	'footsoldier'
fēde-		'foot-'
fæðm	M.	'bosom: embrace; fathom'
feðer, fiðer	MN.	'feather' *pl.* 'wing'
fiðer-		'winged-'; 'four-

F*W
fēawe	adj.*pl.*	'few'
fēower		'four'
fēowertiġ		'forty'

F*X
fox	M.	'fox'
feax	N.	'hair'
fexede	*pp.*	'long-haired'
fix-að		'fishes'
fixas	M*pl.*	'fishes'
fixnoð	M.	'fishing'

G*
ġē	*pl.*	'you'
ġe	conj.	'and, also'
ġe-		prefix with verbs: completion or action taken to conclusion
ġe-		prefix with nouns: = a group
gā		'go!'; gǣð 'goes
ġēa	adv.	'yes'
ġēo	adv.	'formerly, of old, already'

G*C
ġēac	M.	'cuckoo'
ġeoc	N.	'yoke'
ġiċel	Mm.	'icicle'
ġēocend		'saviour'
ġēocor	adj.	'grim, sad'

G*D
gād	N.	'lack, need; goad, point'
ġid(d)	N.	'song, poem, tale'
gōd	adj.	'good': also as subst: 'goodness; a good person'
God	M.	'God'
godcund	adj.	'divine, holy'
ġyden	F.	'goddess'
gōdnes	F.	'goodness'
on-ġeader	adv.	'together'
ġe-gadere	adv.	'together'
gad(e)r-að		'gathers. brings together' *p.* gaderode
gadertang	adv.	'continuous'
god-spell	N.	'gospel'
god-webb		'expensive cloth'

G*F
ġif	conj.	'if'
ġifu	F.	'giving, gift; grace'
ġief-an		'to give' *p.* ġeaf, ġēafon
gafol	N.	'tribute, tax'
ġifol	adj.	'liberal, generous'
gafeluc		'spear, javelin'
ġeofon/ġyfen	N.	'ocean'
ġifen	*pp.*	'given'
ġifende		'giving'
ġīfre	adj.	'greedy, hungry'
ġift	NF.	'marriage-portion, dowry'
ġifeðe	adj.	'allotted, fated, granted'

G*G
ġegnum	adv.	'straight'
ġegnunga	adv.	'instantly; clearly'
ġīgant	M.	'giant'
gag(a)tes		'agate; jet'
ġeoguð	F.	'youth; youngsters'

G*L
gāl	N.	'lust, levity'; adj .'promiscuous'
gal-eð		'sings, chants' *p.* gōl
gǣl-eð		'hinders'
ġēol(a)		'Yule'
ġeolu	adj.	'yellow' gen. geolwes

gōl	p. 'sang, chanted'	ġȳmen	F. 'concern, care'
ġyl-eð	'yells'	ġēomrung	F. 'grief'
ġeol(e)ca	m. 'yolk'	gum-ċyst	F. 'generosity'
onġeald	p. 'paid for'	ġēom(o)r	adj. 'sad, depressing'
ġi(e)ld	N. 'compulsory payment; offering, sacrifice; idol'	ġēomrodep.	'lamented'
ġield-an	'to pay over' ppl. guldon		

G*N

gān	'to go'
ā-gān	pp. 'gone by, passed'
ġe-gān	'to conquer'
be-gān	'to practice, enact'
on-gan	p. 'began'
ġēn	adv. 'yet, still, further, besides'
onġēan	prep/adv. 'opposite'
ġīn-að	'yawns, gapes'
ġinn	adj. 'spacious'
ġeond	prep.+acc. 'throughout, over'
ġeond-	'throughout, thoroughly, too much-'
ġin-fæst	adj.'liberal'
ġeong	adj. 'young'
gang	M. 'travel; circuit'
gang-an	'to go' p. gang/gong
ġenga	m. 'goer'
gang-dagas	Mpl. 'Rogation days'
ġeoniende	'gaping'
ganot	M. 'gannet'

gold	N. 'gold'
gylden	adj. 'golden'
galdor	N. 'song, charm. spell' pl. galdru
gold-wine	M. 'gold-friend, patron'
ġealga	m 'gallows; cross'
ġielp	MN. 'boasting, pride, vanity'
ġielp-eð	'boasts' p. ġealp
gǣlsa	m. 'pride, luxury'
gylt	M. 'guilt, offence'
ġeolwað	'becomes yellow'

GL*

glīu	= glīw 'mirth'
glad-að	'gladdens; rejoices; shines' p. gladode
glad	adj. 'glad' dat.pl. gladum
glēd	F. 'glowing coal, fire'
glīd-eð	'glides, slips' p. glād, glidon
glōf	F. 'glove'
glōma	m. 'twilight'
ġeglengde	pp. 'adorned'
glīdeð/glīt	'glides'
glæs	N. 'glass, glass vessel' pl. glasu
glitnian	II 'to glitter, sparkle'
glēaw	adj. 'clever, perspicacious'
glīw	N. 'glee, fun; music'
glīw-man	M. 'singer (etc)'

GN*

gnīdan	'to crumble (something)'
gnorn	adj. 'sad, depressed'; subst. 'grief'
gnornode p.	'mourned, lamented'

G*P

ġēap	adj. 'spacious, broad'
ġeapsis	'jasper'

G*M

ġim	M. 'gem, jewel' pl. ġimmas
ġīem-eð	'cares for, pays attention'
guma	m. 'man'
gamol	adj. 'aged, greying'
gamen	N. 'sport, amusement, game'

G*R

gār	M. 'spear'
ġēar	NM. 'year'
ġēar-	'yore-; olden'
ġēara	adv. 'of old'
ġeare	adv. = ġearwe 'thoroughly'

[G*R]
ġearo adj. 'prepared. ready'
  gen. ġearwes
ġier-eð 'readies'
ġearcian II 'to prepare, get'
ġeard M. 'yard, residence'
ġierede p. 'readied'
ġyrd F. 'yard, rod'
be-ġyrdan I 'to encase, enlose, surround'
ġirela m. 'dress, outfit'
ġe-arn = arn 'ran'
gurron ppl. 'groaned, creaked'
ġyrnde p. 'yearned (for)' +gen.
ġeorn adj.+gen. 'eager (for)'
ġeorne adv. 'keenly, properly'
gærs N. 'grass'
gār-secg M. 'ocean; ?Neptune'
ġyrstan-dæg 'yesterday'
ġearwa Fpl. 'gear, equipment'
ġearwe adv. 'thoroughly, well, fully' cf. ġearo adj.
ġearwian II 'to prepare, clothe, equip'

GR*
Grēcas Mpl. 'the Greeks'
grēcisc adj. 'Greek'
grǣdiġ adj. 'greedy'
graf-eð 'digs up; engraves' p. grōf
græf N. 'cave, grave
græġ adj. 'grey'
gram adj. 'fierce, threatening'
grem-að 'provokes, annoys'
grīma m. 'mask, helmet'
grim(m) adj. 'fierce, terrible'
grim-eð 'rages'
grom = gram ('angry')
grymetiġ-eð I 'roars, bellows'
grēne adj. 'green'
grēn-að II 'turns green'
grīn NF. 'snare, noose'
grind-eð 'grates. grinds' ppl. grundon
grund M. 'ground, bottom'
grund-lēas adj. 'bottomless'
grund-stan M. 'foundation'
grāp M. 'grip'

grāpað II 'seizes'
gripeð 'grips, seizes' p. ġegrāp
  pp. ġegripen
gryre M. 'a horror, a cause of terror; roughness, violence'
grorn adj. 'sad'; subst. 'sorrow'
græs N. 'grass' pl. grasu
grisliċ adj. 'grisly, horrible'
grēt-eð/grēt 'salutes, greets' p. grētte
grēat adj. 'big'
grēot N. 'grit, sand, earth'
grēot-eð 'weeps'
grið N. 'truce, guarantee of safety'
grōweð/grēwð 'grows' p. grēow
  pp. grōwen

G*S
gōs F. 'goose' pl. gēs
ġīese 'yes'
ġīsl M. 'hostage'
gās-rīċ 'powerful beast'
gāst M. 'spirit, soul; supernatural force'
gast/ġiest M. 'guest, stranger'
gāstliċ adj. 'spiritual, holy'
ġystren- 'yester-'

G*T
gāt F. 'she-goat'
ġeat N. 'gate, opening' pl. gatu
ġēot-eð 'pours out, gushes'
ġīt/ġīeta adv. 'still, yet'
ġit pron. 'you two'
-ġiet-eð 'gets, etc' p. -ġeat - ġēaton
Gota pl.-n 'Goth(s)'
ġyte m. 'outpour, flow'
ġeatoliċ adj. 'magnificent'
ġītsung F. 'avarice, greed'
ġītsere M. 'miser'
ġeatwe Fpl. 'arms, war-gear'

G*TH
gǣð 'goes' p. gang
gūð F. 'combat, war'

H*

hū	adv. 'how'
hē	'he', 'it'
hēa	= hēah 'high'
hēo	'she, it; they'
hī, hīe	nom./acc. 'they'; acc. 'her, it'

H*B

habbað	'have' p. hæfdon
hæbbe	subj. 'might have'
hebbeð	'raises, lifts' p. hōf

H*C

hycgan	'think, consider, etc' p. hogode

H*D

hād	M. 'state, condition, rank, order'
-hād	'condition of—'
ġehād-od	pp. 'in religious orders'
hēd-eð	+gen. 'heeds, observes' ppl. hēddon
behȳd	pp. 'hidden'
hȳd	'hide, skin'
hȳd-an	'to hide something; to tie with a hide rope' ppl. hȳddon
hȳdiġ	= hyġdiġ 'thoughtful'
hādor	adj. 'clear, bright'; subst. 'clearness'
hider	adv. 'hither'

H*F

hæf	N. 'ocean'
hæf-ð	pl. hafað 'has, possesses' ppl. hæfdon
hef-eð	'raises'
hēaf	M. 'wailing'
hēof-eð	'laments' p. hēof
hōf	pl. hōfon 'raised'
hōf	M. 'hoof'
hof	N. 'court, hall'
hȳf	F. 'hive'
hafoc	M. 'hawk'
hēafod	N. 'head' gen. hēafdes
hēafod-	as pref: 'capital-, chief' etc

be-hēafdian	II 'to behead'
hefiġ	adj. 'heavy, serious'
hefigod	pp. 'weighed down'
hafela	m. 'head'
hafen-að	II 'grasps, brandishes'
hæfen	F. 'harbour, haven'
(ā)hæfen/hafen	pp. 'raised, lifted up'
heofon	M. 'heaven(s)'
hafenlēas	adj. 'destitute'
hæft	M. 'fetter'; adj. 'captive'
ġehæfted	pp. 'chained, captured'
hæfð	'has, possesses' (habban)

H*G

haga	m. 'hedge, enclosure'
ġehæġ	N. 'field, meadow'
hiġ	= hī 'they; them'
hyġe	M. 'thought; mind, attitude'
hyġ-eð	'thinks about' (hycgan)
hogode	'thought of, was busy with' (hogian)
hyġd	FN. 'mind'
hyġdiġ	adj. 'thoughtful, nice'
hagol	MN. 'hail'
hagosteald	adj./subst. 'unmarried, of military age'

H*H

hēah	adj. 'high; deep'
hēah-	'chief, arch-, great'
ġehōh	'hang, suspend!'
hēhst/hȳhst	adj. 'highest'
hēhst	'hangs up'
hēht	'is called; orders'
hyht	MF 'hope, trust'
hēhðo	F. 'height; the heavens'

H*L

hāl	adj. 'healthy, whole'
hǣl-eð	I 'cures, heals'
hǣlu/hǣl	F. 'health, salvation'
hæle	M. 'man'
hell/helle	Ff. 'Hell'
hel-eð	'conceals'
heall	F. 'hall, palace'
hol	adj. 'hollow'; subst. 'a cave'

[H*L]
hēalic̀ adj. 'exalted, noble'
ġehealdsumnes F. 'custom; fast'
hild F. 'warfare, combat'
(ā)hild *pp*. 'bent, laid down'
hold adj. 'loyal, friendly'
hyldu F. 'favour, kind notice'
healdeð 'holds, possesses, contains' *p*. heold
heldeð 'inclines, leans
healf F. 'half; side'
heolfer N. 'gore'
hālga adj. 'holy'; subst. 'saint'
haliġ adj. 'holy'
ġehālgod *pp*. 'hallowed, saintly'
helm M. 'cover, lid, helmet, crown of a tree; protector, leader'
helm-að 'covers'
helma m. 'helm, rudder'
holm M. 'sea'
Hǣlend M. 'Saviour i.e. Christ'
help FM 'help'
helpeð/hilpð 'helps'
huilpe f. 'sea-bird, curlew'
heals M. 'neck; prow'
healsað 'implores'
heolstor M. 'darkness, invisibility'
hilt M. 'hilt'
holt M. 'forest, wood'
hylt 'holds; leans'
hǣleð M. 'man, hero'
hāl-wende adj. 'salutary'

HL*
hlēo = hlēow 'shelter'
hlad-eð 'he loads, draws' *p*. hlēod, hlād(on) *pp*. ġehlǣden
hlid-on *ppl*. 'they arose, appeared'
hlūd adj. 'loud, noisy'
hlȳdeð 'is noisy'
hlǣder F. 'ladder'
hlāf M. 'loaf'
hlǣfdiġe F. 'lady, woman of status'
hlāford M. 'lord'
hlifað II 'towers up
ā-hlōg *p*. 'laughed'

hleahtor M. 'laughter'
hlimman I 'to resound'
hlinað 'leans, reclines' *p*. hlynode
hlyneð 'shouts' *p*. hlynede
be-hlǣneð 'surrounds'
hlynsode *p*. 'echoed, resounded'
hlēapeð 'leaps' *p*. hlēop
hlēor N. 'cheek, face'
hlīsa m. 'sound; reputation'
hlæst N. 'load, cargo'
hlēotan 'to cast lots; get, obtain' *ppl*. hluton
hlott N. '(selection by) lot, portion'
hlūt(t)or adj. 'bright, clear'
hlið N. 'cliff, slope' *pl*. hleoðu
hlōð F. 'crowd, troop; booty'
hlēoðor N. 'noise; voice'
hlēoðrode*p*. 'spoke'
hlǣw MN '(burial) mound, hill'
hlēow MN 'shelter, refuge'

H*M
hām M. 'home, household, village'
hamm M. 'pasture-land, water-land'
hama m. 'coating, cover. 'skin"
him '(to) him, it, them'
hǣmed N. 'sexual intercourse, adultery' *pl*. hǣmedru

H*N
hēan adj. 'lowly, pitiful'
hēan, hēanne = hēah 'high'
henn F. 'hen'
hīen-eð 'humiliates' *p*. hȳnde
hōn 'to hang [someone]'
hancrēd M. 'cockcrow'
hand/hond F. 'hand; ownership, position, etc'
ġehende +*dat* 'close, handy'
(ġe)hend-eð 'catches'
hind F. 'female deer, hind'
hund M. 'hound, dog'
hund N. 'a hundred'

hund-	prefix of numbers between 60 and 120	her-eð	I 'praises' (herian)
hond-bred	'palm'hinder adj./adv. 'after, behind, back'	hēore	adj. 'agreeable'
		heora	'their, of them'
hundred	N. '100; a local court'	heoru	M. 'sword'
hond-ġesella	m. 'companion'	hire/hyre	'hers, to her'
hin-fūs	adj. 'keen to get away'	hīerra	adj. 'higher. superior'
hang-að	'hangs, dangles; hangs [someone]' p. heng pp. ġehangen	hūru	adv, 'however, yet'
		hȳr-eð	I 'hears, listens to, obeys'
		ġehȳr-að	I 'obeys'
huniġ	N. 'honey'	heard	adj. 'hard, stern'
hungor	M. 'hunger'	hīred	M. 'household, group'
hungriġ	adj. 'hungry'	hord	gen. -es 'treasure-hoard'
hēanlic	adj. 'humiliating'	hyrde	M. 'shepherd'
heonon	adv. 'hence'	heard-mōd	adj. 'bold: obstinate'
hēaness	F. 'highness'		
hin-sīð	M. 'going hence, death'	heriġe	obl.of here 'army'
hent-an	'to pursue; lay hold of'	hǣring	M. 'herring'
hunta	m. 'huntsman'	hord-ern	N. 'treasury, store-room'
hunt(n)oðM. 'hunting'		hærfest	M. 'harvest-time, autumn'
huntēontiġ	'one hundred'		
hīenð(u)	F. 'humiliation'	heriġean	'to praise'
		herg-að	'raids'
HN*		hergung	F. 'pillage'
hine	acc. 'him, it'	here-ġeatu	'war-tax'
hnǣġed	pp. 'humbled, vanquished'	hearm	M. 'injury, damage'
		horn	M. 'musical or drinking horn'
hnīġeð	'bends, bows' pp. hniġen		
hnol	M. 'top of head'	hyrned	pp. 'horned'
hnipað	'bends,'inclines the head'	hearpe	f. 'harp'
hnesce	adj. 'soft, mild; enervated'	hors	N. 'horse' pl. hors
		horsc	adj. 'sharp, cunning'
ġe-hnǣst	N. 'conflict'	ġehȳrsum+dat. 'obedient'	
hnītan	'to gore, clash' ppl. hniton	ġehorsian II 'to provide with horses'	
		hyrst	F. 'decoration, article of value'
hnutu	F. 'nut'		
		heorte	f. 'heart, disposition'
H*P		heorot	M. 'hart, stag'
hēap	MF 'crowd, band'	here-toga m. 'general. consul'	
hop	N. 'swampy area'	heorð	M. 'hearth; home'
hop-að	'hopes, trusts in'		
hōpiġ	adj. 'bouncy'	**HR***	
		hrā	= hrǣw 'corpse, body'
H*R		hrycg	M. 'spine, ridge'
hār	adj. 'grey & ancient'	hreddan	'to rescue'
hara	m. 'hare'	hræd	adj. 'quick, alert' dat.pl. hradum
hēr	adv. 'here'		
here	M. 'raiding army' dat. herġe	hrædlīċe adv. 'quickly'	
		ġehroden pp. 'adorned'	
		hrēof	adj. 'rough, scaley'

[HR*]
M. 'roof, ceiling'
hrefn M. 'raven'
hrægl N. 'clothing; armour'
hrēoh adj. 'rough, fierce, stormy'
hrēam M. 'alarm, outcry'
hrīm M. 'rime, hoar-frost'
hrīem-eð 'shouts'
hrēmiġ adj. 'boastful'
hremming F. 'obstacle'
hremmas M*pl.* 'ravens'
hrān M. 'reindeer'; *p.*'he touched'
hrēone *acc.*M. of hrēoh 'rough'
hrīn-eð 'touches' *p.* hrān
hron/hran M. 'whale'
hrinde adj. 'hoary'
hring M. 'ring, circuit'
hrepsung 'evening'
hrōpende 'yelling' *ppl.* hrēopon
hrēran 'to shake' *ppl.* hrērdon
hrōr adj. 'active, agile'
hruron *ppl.* 'fell down'; *pp.* ġehroren
hryre M. 'fall, ruin'
hrǣs *gen.*of hrēaw 'corpse'
hrēoseð/hrēst/hrīst 'sinks, falls down' *p.* hrēas
hrūse f. 'earth, ground'
hrysted *pp.* = hyrsted 'decorated'
hraðe adv. 'quickly, promptly'
hrēð MN. 'victory'
hrēðiġ 'exultant'
hreðer M. 'breast; heart, mind'
hrīðer N. 'ox, bull etc'
hraðost superl. 'quickest'
hrǣw/hrēaw 'corpse' *gen.* hrǣs
hrēow F. 'sorrow, repentance'
hrēowsian II 'to repent'

H*S
hās adj. 'hoarse'
hasu adj. 'grey, ash-coloured'
hǣs F. 'request'
his 'his, of him; its, of it'
hūs N. 'house'
hys = 'his/is'

hyse M. 'son, young man' *pl.* hyssas
hūsc/hūx N. 'scorn, ridicule'
hūsel N. 'the host (Holy Communion)'
hosp M. 'abuse, insult'
hǣst adj. 'violent'
haswiġ- 'grey-' cf hasu

H*T
hāt adj. 'hot'
hātte 'is called'
hāt-að 'heats up'
hāt-eð 'is called; orders'
hat-að II 'hates'
hǣt-eð 'heats'
hǣtt *p.* 'ordered'
hǣtu F. 'heat'
hēte *p.* 'you commanded': hēt 'he commanded'
hete M. 'hate'
hīt 'hides' (hȳdan)
hit 'it'
hāt-heort adj. 'passionate, angry'
hatol/hetol adj. 'hostile'
hetelīċe adv. 'hatefully, violently'
ġehāten *pp* '(is) called; ordered'
hatung F. 'hatred'

H*TH
hǣð N. 'heathland'
heaðo-/heaðu- pref. 'war, battle'
hūð F. 'booty, quarry'
hȳð F. 'harbour, landing-place'
hȳðan 'to plunder'
hǣðen adj. 'heathen'

H*W
hāw-að II 'gazes on, notices'
hēow *p.* 'cut down' *pp.* ġehēawen
hīw/hēow N. 'colour; appearance, type'
hīwan *pl.* 'members of family, household'
hīw-að 'fashions, forms' *p.* hēowade *pp.* ġehīwod
hǣwen adj. 'bluish, purply'

HW*
hwā	'who, what; anyone'
ġehwā	'every(one)'
hwī	'why'
ġehwæde adj.	'insignificant'
hwider	'whither'
hwæl	M. 'whale' *pl.* hwalas
hwēol	N. 'wheel'
hwīl	F. 'a time, a while'
hwelċ/hwilċ	'which: whatever'
ġehwilċ	'each, every'
hwealf	F. 'arch, vault' also adj.
hwīlum/hwīlon adv.	'sometimes'
hwelpas	*pl.* 'cubs'
hwamm/hwemm	M. 'corner'
hwǣm	*dat.* of hwā
hwēne	adv. 'a little'
hwōn	adj/subst. 'a little'
hwon	'by which'
tō hwon/for hwon	'for what, why'
hwonne/hwænne	'when'
hwanon	'whence'
hwēop	*p.* 'threatened'
hwǣr	'where'
ġehwǣr	'everywhere'
hwearf	*p.* 'turned'
hwyrfð/hwearfað	'revolves, exists, changes'
hwurfon/hwearfodon *ppl.*	'turned'
hwæs	'whose'
hwistlung F.	'whistling, hissing'
hwæt	'what!; what...?'
hwæt	adj. 'bold, active'
hwǣte	M. 'wheat'
hwet-eð	'whets, incites; is keen'
hwīt	adj. 'white, bright'
hwæt-hwugu	'somewhat'
-hwatan	*pl.* suff. '-heroes'
hweoðu	F. 'breeze'
hwæðer	'whether'; ġehwæðer 'both'
hwæðre	adv. 'nonetheless, yet'
hweowul	N. 'wheel'

L*
lā	'lo!'
lēo	Mm. 'lion'

L*B
libban	'to live' *p.* lifede
lyb-lāc	MN 'magic, spellwork'

L*C
lāc-eð	'vibrates, makes play with; flies'
lāc	N. 'sacrifice, offering'
ġelāc	N. 'play: chaos: offering'
lacu	F. 'stream, pond'
lǣċe	M. 'doctor'
læċ-eð	'captures'
lēac	N. 'plant, herb, leek'
līċ	N. 'body; corpse'
līc-að	+*dat.* 'it pleases someone'
ġelīċ	adj. 'like, similar to' +*dat.*
ġelīca	subst. 'an equal, a similar'
ġelīċe	adv. 'likewise'
-līċ/-līċe etc.	(suffix) '-like; -ly'
lōc-ian	'look, gaze' *p.* lōcade
loca	m. 'closed place; stronghold'
lȳc-ð	'shuts or locks up; excludes' *pp.* locen
lǣċedom	M. 'healing'
lecgan	'to lay, position, arrange'
licgan	'to lie down, be at rest, extend'
līċ-hama	m. 'body, bodily shell'
līċhamlīċ	adj. 'physical'
lācn-að	II 'heals. cures'
lācnung	F. 'healing, remedy'
ġelīċnyss	F. 'likeness'
an-līost	adj. +*dat.* 'most like (to)'

L*D
lād	F. 'course, way, street'
lǣd-eð	'leads, brings' *p.* lǣdde, lǣddon
lead	N. 'lead (metal)'
lēod	M. 'man'
lēode	F *pl.* 'nation, people'
lēod-	'of one's country; general-'
lid	N. 'ship'
lida	m. 'sailor'
Lǣden	'Latin'
Lǣdenware	M *pl.* 'the Romans'

[LeicestershireD]
lid-mon M. 'sailor'
ġe-liden pp. 'sailed, travelled'
(h)loden pp. 'laden'
(h)lædder F. 'ladder'
lādðēow/lāttēow 'leader'

L*F
lāf F. 'remnant, remains'
læf-eð 'leaves behind, bequeaths' p. læfde
lēf adj. 'feeble, precarious'
lēf pl. 'loaves'
lēaf M. 'leaf
lēaf F. 'permission'
ġelēafa m. 'faith, belief'
lēof adj. 'dear, beloved'
leof-að 'lives' p. leofede
līf N. 'life'
līef-eð 'allows, entrusts' p. (ā)lȳfde
(ġe)līef-eð/ġelȳfð 'believes' sim. belīefeð
lof N. 'praise'
lufu Ff. 'love'
luf-að 'loves' p. lufode
(ā)lēfed pp. 'injured, ill'
ġelȳfed adj. 'advanced in age'
līf-dagas M pl. 'lifetime'
lifi(ġ)ende 'living'
lyft 'air, atmosphere, sky'

L*G
laga F pl. 'laws'
lagu F. 'water'
læġ 'lay' pl. lægon
lēag p. 'lied; lent'
lēog-an 'to lie, betray, deceive'
līġ/lēġ MN 'fire; lightning'
leġ-eð 'lays' (lecgan)
liġ-eð 'lies, reclines' (licgan)
ġelōg-að II 'arranges; lodges'
leġer N. 'bed, repose; grave'
līġet(u) 'lightning'

L*H
lah- 'law-'
ġelæht pp. 'caught'
leahte p. 'moistened'

lēoht N. 'light': also adj. 'light'
līht-eð 'lightens; illuminates'
līhting F. 'illumination'
leahtor M. 'vice, sin'
leahtriċ M. 'lettuce'

L*L
lilie f. 'lily'
(be)leolc p. 'made sway' (lācan)

L*M
lām N. 'clay, earth'
lēoma m. 'gleam. light' pl. lēoman
līm M. 'sticky lime; trap'
lim N. 'limb (of a tree etc) pl. leomu
ġelōma m. 'tool'
ġelōme adj./adv. 'often, frequent(ly)'
ġelimpeð 'happens, comes about' p. ġelomp pp. ġelumpen
ġelimpliċ adj. 'appropriate'

L*N
læne adj. 'temporary, transient, perishable, frail'
lēan N. 'reward'
lēan-ian 'to reward'
lēon obl. 'lion'; sim. lēona
līne f. 'line'
linn-an 'to lose' +dat.
lencten M. 'springtime'
lind M. '(linden-wood) shield'
lond/land N. 'land'
Lunden-byriġ F. 'London'
lange adv. 'for a long time'
ġelang adj. 'dependent'
leng F. 'length. height'
leng/lencg adv. 'longer'
ġeleng-an 'to protract
lang-fǣre adj. 'long-enduring'
lungre adv. 'quickly'
langsum adj. 'lasting, tedious'
lent/lendeð 'lands, ends up, goes'

L*P
lopystran f.pl. 'lobsters'

L*R
lār	F. 'learning; advice'
lǣr-eð	'teaches' *p.* lǣrde
tō lore	'to the end, to destruction'
ġelǣred	adj. 'educated'
(for)lorenpp.	'lost'
leorn-ian	'learn, study' *p.* heornode
leornung	F. 'learning'
leorneras	M*pl.* 'disciples; scholars'
lārēow	M. 'teacher'

L*S
lǣs	adv. 'less'; ðȳ lǣs þe 'lest'
lǣssa	adj. 'less, smaller'
lēas	adj. 'false'; +*gen.* 'free (of)'
-lēas	'without'
(ā)līes-eð	'releases' *pp.* lȳsed
liss	F. 'grace, kindness'
losian	'to fail, die; escape'
lēasung	F. 'lie, fiction'
lēasere	M. 'liar, hypocrite'
lāst	M. 'foot-print, track'
lǣst	superl. 'least'
lǣst-eð	'achieves, carries out, endures'
list	'skill, cleverness'
lust	M. 'desire'
lyst-eð	'it pleases someone (to...)'
lust-bǣre	adj. 'desirable, pleasant'
lust-līċe	adv. 'willingly'
lustum	adv. 'gladly'
lǣswe	*obl.* 'pasture'

L*T
lǣt	'he leads; he left'
lǣt-an	'to allow, permit: leave behind, let out' *p.* lēt
onlǣt-an	'to relax (something)'
forlǣt-eð	'abandons'
læt	adj. 'late, tardy'
lett-an	'to hinder, impede' *ppl.* letton
lot	N. 'trickery'
lūt-an	'to bend, bow'
lūt-ian	II 'to lie hidden, lurk'
lytiġ	adj. 'cunning'
lȳtel	adj. 'little'
lȳtl-að	II 'lessens, shortens'
(ā)lȳten	*pp.* 'bent over'
lator, latost	adj. 'later... latest'
(h)lūtt(o)radj.	'clear'
lāttēow	M. 'leader'

L*TH
lāð	adj./subst. 'loathesome, nasty'
lað-að	II 'invites'
lēoð	N. 'song, poem'
līðe	adj. 'gentle, sweet'
līð-eð/līð	'travels, sails'
līð	'lies down' (= liġeð)
lið	N. 'limb' *pl.* leoðu
līðigað	'softens, calms'
ġelaðung	F. 'community'
leðer	M. 'leather'
lȳðre	adj. 'wicked, corrupt'

L*W
lǣwede	adj. 'lay (man)'

L*X
lēax	M. 'salmon'
līx-eð	'shines' *p.* līxte

M*
mā	adj./adv. 'more'
mē	*acc./dat.* 'me, to me'

M*C
mac-að	II 'makes' *p.* macode
ġemæċċa	'mate, match' *pl.* -n
mēċe	'sword'
meċ	*acc.* 'me'
mæcg	M. 'man; son'
miċel	adj. 'great, much'
miċlade	*p.* 'increased'
miċlum	adv. 'greatly'

M*D
mǣd	F. 'meadow' *pl.* mǣd(w)a
mēd	F. 'reward'
medu	'mead' *gen.* medwes
[M*D]	

mid prep. '(together) with, among, by': mid þām þe 'when, while'
midde adj./subst. 'middle'
mōd N. 'mind, disposition, courage'
ofer-mōd 'pride, overconfidence'
mōdiġ adj. 'haughty, brave'
mōdiġ(i)an 'to become proud; be brave; show anger'
mōd-ġeþanc M. 'thought, mind'
mādmas pl. = māðmas 'treasures
medeme, medemliċ, medmiċel adj. 'middling, average'
onmiddan/onmiddum 'in the middle of'
midl N. 'middle, centre'
medmiċel adj. 'moderate'
mǣden N. 'maiden'
middan-ġeard M. 'the world'
mōdor F. 'mother' dat. mēder
mōd-sefa m. 'heart, mind'
medtrumnes F. 'weakness, disability'
medwes gen. of medu 'mead'

M*G
māga m. 'son'
mago M. 'son, kinsman' pl. mæcgas
mǣġ M. 'kinsman, relation' pl. māgas
mæġ 'he can' pl. magon
mæġden N. 'maiden'
meagol adj. 'strong, determined, confident'
magon 'they can'
mæġen N. 'strength, power; a troop'
mæġen- 'huge, mighty-'
magister M. 'master'
mǣġð F. 'clan, race'
mæġð F. 'maiden, wife'
mæġð-hād M. 'virginity'
mæġ-wlite M. 'form, species'

M*H
ġemāgliċ adj. 'impudent'
miht/meaht F. 'power, force'

mihte/meahte p. 'might, could' pl. meah ton
mihtiġ adj. 'mighty, important'

M*L
mǣl N. 'mark, sign (e.g. cross); time, occasion'
mǣl-eð 'speaks, talks' p. mǣlde
mīl F. 'a mile'
meolc F. 'milk'
meld-ode p. 'announced, proclaimed'
milde adj. 'merciful, considerate'
molde f. 'soil; the earth'
mylen 'mill'; —hwēowul 'millwheel'
mildsian II 'take pity on'
mealt p. 'melted' pl. multon
milts F. 'compassion'

M*N
mān N. 'crime'
mān- 'evil-'
ġemāna m. 'community, communication'
man(n) M. 'human, man' pl. men
man 'one' in 'one likes to...' etc.
ġeman pl. ġemunon +gen. 'considers, remembers' p. ġemunde
ġemǣne adj. 'in common'
unġemǣn adj. 'unusual'
mǣn-eð I 'means, signifies; mentions; bemoans'
mīn adj. 'my, mine'
mōna m. 'the moon'
mon-að II 'urges' p. monade
myne M. 'affection, feeling'
myn-að 'intends, aims to, considers' p. mynte
munuc M. 'monk'
moncyn N. 'mankind'
mancus M. 'silver coin'
munuc-hād M. 'monastic order'
ġemanode p. 'instructed, encouraged'

mund   F. 'hand; protector,
                protection'
ġemunde p. 'remembered'
ġemynd   N. 'thought, mind;
                memory'
ġemynde/ġemyndiġ adj. 'mindful
                (of)'
mundbora   m. 'protector,
                officer'
ġemyndgað   II 'remembers'
mānful   adj. 'wicked'
ġemang   N. 'mixture; multitude'
ġemeng-ed   pp. 'mixed'
moniġ/maniġ   adj. 'many'
menigo, mængeo   F. 'crowd, host'
maniġfeald   adj. 'various'
mennisc   adj. 'human'
mynster   N. 'monastery, minster'
mynsterlic   adj. 'monastic'
munt   M. 'mountain'
mynte   p. 'intended, aimed to'
man-þwǣre   adj. 'gentle,
                merciful'
mōnað/mōnð   M. 'month' pl.
                mōnðas

M*R
māra   adj. 'greater, more'
mǣre   adj. 'famous'
mǣr-eð   'glorifies; delimits'
ġemǣre   N. 'boundary; territory'
mēra   gen.pl. of mearh ('horse')
mere   M. 'sea; lake'
mōr   M. 'moor, morass'
mȳre   f. 'a mare'
mearc   F. 'mark, boundary, area'
myrce   adj. 'murky'
mearg/mearh   M. 'a horse' gen.
                meares
myrġe   adj. 'pleasant'
morgen   M. 'morning; tomorrow'
meregrotan   pl. 'pearls'
mearh   - see mearg, above
marmor-stān   M. 'marble'
murn-an. murn-ð   'to mourn /
                mourns'
mǣrs-að   II 'praises, exalts'
mēares - see mearg
mersc   M. 'marsh'

mere-swīn   N. 'porpoise,
                dolphin'
martirdom   M. 'martyrdom'
morð(or) M. 'murder, grave crime'
myrġð   F. 'mirth, pleasure'
mǣrðu   F. 'marvel, glory'

M*S
mæsse   f. 'mass (holy
                communion)'
mis-   'wrongly, mis-'
muscle   f. 'mussel' pl. muslan
misdǣd   F. 'misdeed'
mislic   adj. 'unalike, varied'
missenlic adj. 'various'
misser   M. 'a season'
mǣst   adj./adv 'most'
mæst   M. 'mast'
-mest   '-most'
mist   M. 'mist'
mōste   mōston p. 'might, were
                allowed to'
must   M. 'raw wine'
mæstling N. 'brass'

M*T
ġemǣte   adj. 'suitable'
ġemǣtte   p. 'came in dream'
ġemǣte   adj. 'small'
mæt   p. 'measured'
mēt-eð   I 'meet, come across'
met-eð   'measures out'; sim.
                āmetan
āmet   pp. 'painted, studded'
mete, mæte   M. 'food' pl. mettas
ġemet   adj. 'appropriate'; subst.
                'a measure(ment)'
mitte (ðe) 'when, while'
mōt   pl. mōton 'may, is
                allowed to'
ġemōt   N. 'moot, judicial
                assembly; encounter'
Me(o)tod M. 'God (as regulator of
                the universe)'
ġemetfǣst adj. 'reasonable'
metg-að   'moderates, controls,
                restrains' p. metgode
ġemetgung   F. 'moderation'
ġemetlīce adv. 'moderately'

Metend 'God (as layer-out of the universe)'

M*TH
mēð/mǣðF. 'rate; proportion; rightness, capability'
mēðe adj. 'tired'
mīð-eð 'hides, avoids'
mūð M. 'mouth'
mæðel N. 'council, discussion'
maðel-að 'speaks out' *p.* maðelode
māð(u)m M. 'treasure, precious object'

M*W
māw-an 'to mow
mēaw/mǣw M. 'seagull'
mēowle f. 'woman

M*X
max N. 'net'
meox N. 'dung, dirt'

N*
nā/nō adv. 'not, not at all'
ne adv. 'not'; conj. 'nor'
nū adv. 'now

N*B
nabb-að 'has not, lacks' *p.* næfde
nebb N. 'bill, beak'

N*C
naca m. 'boat'
nić 'not I'
nacod adj. 'naked'
nicor M. 'water-spirit or monster' *pl.* nicras

N*D
nēod F. 'desire, zeal'
nēde adv. 'necessarily'
nēad-að, nīed-eð 'compels'
nīed FN. 'necessity, compulsion'
nīed-behēfe adj. 'necessary'
nēod-fracu F. 'greed'
nǣdl F. 'needle'
nēodlīċe adv. 'eagerly'

nǣdre f. 'adder, snake'
nīed-ðearf F. 'necessity; lack'

N*F
nafu F. 'nave (of a wheel)'
naf-að/nāfð 'has not' *p.* næfde
nefa m. 'nephew, cousin'
nafola m. 'navel, centre'
nǣfre adv. 'never'

N*G
ġenōg adj. 'enough'
ġenǣġed *pp.* 'attacked'
nǣġl M. 'nail'
nigon 'nine'

N*H
nāh 'has not' *p.* nāhte
nēah adj. 'near, nearly'
ġenēah, ġenōh adj. 'enough'
nēhst adj. 'nearest: latest (of time)'
nīehsta m. 'neighbour'
æt nēhstan 'eventually, in due course'
nāhte *p.* 'had not, lacked'
nāuht, nāht adv. 'not at all; nothing'
niht/neahtF. 'night; 24-hours; darkness'
ġenyht FN 'abundance'
ġenihtsum adj. 'plentiful'
ġenihtsum-að 'suffices, abounds'
niht-wacoF. 'night-watches'
nā-hwǣr adv. 'nowhere, no way'

N*L
nēol = neowol 'precipitous, headfirst'
nele/nyle, nellað 'does not wish (to)' *p.* nolde
nēalǣċeð/nēalǣhð 'approaches, comes close' *p.* nēalǣhte
nēalīċe adv. 'nearly'
nalæs, nealles adv. 'not at all'

N*M
nam *p.* 'took'
for-nam *p.* 'destroyed'

88

nama	m. 'name'	nese	adv. 'no'
nim-ð	'takes, obtains' p.	nēos-að	II 'seeks out, attacks'
	nam/nom, nāmon pp. ġenumen	nosu	F. 'nose'
		nāst	'knows not'
nemn-an	'to name, call' p. nemde pp. ġenemnod	nest	N. 'nest'
		nyste	p. 'did not know'
nemne	conj. 'unless'	nos-þyrl	N. 'nostril'
nymðe	conj. 'except, unless'		

N*N

nān, nǣnne etc. pron/adj 'none, no one'
nēan   adv. '(from) nearby'
nōn   'mid-afternoon; church service of nones'
nunne f. 'nun'
nǣniġ adj./pron. 'no one, none'
nānuht adv./pron. 'nothing, not at all'
nānwuht = nānuht

N*P

nīpan   'to darken' p. nāp
nīpende   'darkening'
ġenip   N. 'darkness, obscurity'

N*R

nǣre   pl. nǣron 'was not, were not'
ner-eð   'saves' p. nerede
nēar   adj. 'nearer'
nearu   adj. 'oppressive, narrow' subst. 'danger, difficulty' pl. nearwe
nerġend   M. 'saviour, Christ'
norð, norðerne adj. 'northern'
norðan   adv. 'from the north'
Norð(an)hymbre Mpl. 'Northumbrians'
nearwe   adv. 'closely, tightly' (= nearu)
nearw-ian 'to confine'
for-nearwian 'to become unproductive'
neorxna-wang M. 'Paradise'

N*S

nǣs   'was not' pl. nǣron
nǣss M. 'headland, cliff'

N*T

nāt   'does not know, is ignorant of' pl. nyton
nett   N. 'net'
nēat   N. 'cattle'
neot-eð/notað 'uses, enjoys' +gen.
nytt   adj. 'useful' subst. 'use; function'
nyt-an   'not to know'
nāt-hwā   adj.,'pron. 'some one'
nāt-hwilċ adj./pron. 'some sort or other'
nȳten   N. 'animal'
nytenness F. 'ignorance'
nyttnes   F. 'usefulness'
nytente   'shining'
nāteshwōn, nātoþæshwōn adv. 'by no means, not at all'
nyt-wyrðe adj. 'notable'

N *TH

ġenēð-eð 'risks, ventures on' p. nēðde
nīð   M. 'violence, hatred'
niððas   Mpl. 'men'
nōð   F. 'daring; plunder'
ġeniðla   m. 'foe'
nȳðemest adj. 'lowest'
neoðan   adv. '(from) below, beneath'
nāðer   'neither'
niðer   adv. 'below, downwards'

N*W

nīwe   adj. 'new, fresh'
nāwiht   = nāht 'nothing, not at all'
neowol   adj. 'precipitous'
niwelnyss F. 'chasm'
nīwan   adv. 'recently'

[N*W]
nāwār adv. 'nowhere'
nēawest F. 'neighbourhood'

N*X
nȳxtan = nīehstan 'nearest, last'

P*C
(be)pǣċ-eð 'seduces, perverts'
piċ N. 'pitch'
pīċ M. 'point, pick'

P*D
-pād '-coat, outer covering'

P*L
pæll M. 'purple cloak'
pīl M. 'spike, dart'
pyle 'pillow'
palm(a) 'palm-tree

PL*
plega m. 'quick movement, activity, celebration'
pleġeð 'sports, plays' p. plegode
pleo(h) N. 'peril, danger' gen. plēos
plantian II 'to plant out'

P*N
pīn-að 'tortures'
pun-ode p. 'pounded'
pund N. 'a pound (weight/money)'
pīn-bēam M. 'pine-tree'
pīnn-hnutu F. 'pine-cone'
pening M. 'penny, coin'

P*P
pāpa m. 'Pope'
pīp-drēam M. 'organ music'

P*R
pearruc M. 'park, enclosed land'
pardus pl. 'leopards'
purpure f. 'purple (cloth)'
port MN. 'port, harbour-town'

PR*
prica m. 'point, spot; small radius or time ('degree')'
pric-að I 'pricks, stings'
prass M. 'pomp
prēost M. 'priest'
prȳto F. 'pride, arrogance'
prēowt-hwīl F. 'blink of an eyelid'

P* S
pistol M. 'letter; epistle'
postol M. 'apostle'

P*T
pytt M. 'pit, hole'

P*TH
pæð M. 'path' pl. paðas
peðð-eð I 'treads, walks'

R*
rā m. 'roebuck'

R*C
racu F. 'narration, speech'
rǣċ-an 'to reach out, offer' p. rǣhte
ġerǣċan 'to reach, seize, obtain, control'
rēċ M. 'smoke'
ġereċ N. 'rule, government; directive; an uproar'
reċeð 'brings, proffers'
reċċan, recċeð 'to relate; decide; stretch, extend; care about' p. reahte
rēoc-eð 'smokes, steams'
rīċe N. 'power: kingdom'; adj: 'strong, powerful, rich'
reċed NM. 'hall'
ġereċednis F. 'narrative'
reċlīċe adv. 'orderly, straightforwardly, directly'
ġereċlīċe adv. 'in a straight or orderly way'
rēċe-lēas adj. 'reckless, careless'
rēċels M. 'incense'

reċene	adv. 'promptly'		**R*H**	
reċċend	M. 'ruler'		rūh	adj. 'rough, shaggy' *gen.* rūwes
racente	f. 'chain'		ġeræhte	*p.* 'reached' (ræċan)
rīcsað	'rules, reigns' *p.* rīcsode		rehte	*p.* 'cared about' (reċċan/rēċan)

R*D
rād	*p.* 'rode' (rīdan)
rād	F. 'riding, journey; raid'
ġerād	N. 'assesment, discernment: condition': adj. 'adapted, special'
ræd	M. 'advice; wisdom; benefit'
ræd-eð	'reads'
ġeræded	'advises, designs, arranges'
ġerædu	N*pl.* 'trappings'
ġeræde	adj. 'prepared'
(ā)rēde	*p.* 'he read'
rēad	adj. 'red, orange'
rīd-eð	'rides' *p.* rēd, ridon
rōd	F. 'cross, rood'
ræd-bora	m. 'counsellor'
rædliċ	adj. 'advisable, sensible'
rædels	'riddle'
rædend	M. 'controller, director'
rīdend	M. 'rider'
ræding	F. 'a reading; thinking over'
rodor	M. 'sky, firmament' *gen.* rodres
radost	= hraðost 'speediest'

R*F
rēaf	N. 'plunder'; 'clothing'
(be)rēaf-að	'robs, plunders' *p.* berēafode
ġerēfa	m. 'reeve, official, sheriff'
rōf	adj. 'strong, heroic'
rȳfe	adj. 'rife'
rēafere	M. 'thief'

R*G
regol	M '(monastic) regulation'
reġn/rēn	M. 'rain'
ġereġnad	adj. 'decorated'

reht	= reċċeð 'decides, rules'
reahte/rehte	*p.* 'stretched; narrated, told' (reċċan)
riht	adj. 'right, correct, etc'; subst. N. 'right, justice, truth'
riht-	'proper, lawful, orthodox'
rihte	adv. 'truly, straight, etc'
riht-eð	I 'puts right; governs'
rihtend	M. 'director, ruler'
riht-wīs	adj. 'righteous, just, pious'

R*M
ramm	M. 'a ram (animal)'
ġerīm	N. 'number, reckoning, count'
(ā)rīm-an	I 'reckon up'
rima	m. 'rim, coast'
Rōm	F. 'Rome'
rūm	adj. 'spacious; generous'
ġerūme	adv. 'widely, amply'
rȳm-an	'to expand, clear, open up' *p.* rȳmde
rūm-heort	adj. 'generous'
Rōmane	*pl.* 'Romans'

R*N
rān	*obl.* of rā 'roebuck'
rēn	M. 'rain'
ġerēne	N. 'ornament'
ren-	'hall-'
rīn-eð	'it rains'
rin-eð	'runs' *p.* ran
rūn	F. 'secret; private talk; a rune'
rȳn	'to growl, roar'
ġerūne	N. 'mystery'
ryne/rene	MN 'course, orbit, movement'
ranc	adj. 'proud, noble, bold'
rinc	M. 'warrior, man'
rūn-cofa	m. 'bosom, heart'

[R*N]
rand M. 'round shield'
ġerēnod pp. 'arranged, set'
rind(e) F. 'bark (of tree)'
rēoniġ adj. 'gloomy'
rūn-wita m. 'wise man, adviser'

R*P
rīp N. 'harvest'
rīpe adj. 'ripe'
rīp-að 'ripens' (rīpian)
rīp-eð 'reaps' (rīpan)
rȳp-eð 'robs, plunders' *p.* rȳpte
repsung F. 'evening'

R*R
rǣr-eð 'rears, raises' *p.* rǣrde
reord FN. 'voice'; 'food'
reord-að 'speaks'
reord-berend M. 'voice-bearer, man'

R*S
rǣs M. '(on)rush'
rǣs-an 'to rush at, attack' *p.* rǣsde
rīs-eð/rīst 'rises up; suits, fits' *p.* (ā)rās
rōse f. 'rose'
rysel M. 'lard; resin'
ġerisenliċ adj. 'suitable, decent'
rāsettan 'to rage (of fire)'
rest F. 'sleep, rest; bed'
rest-eð 'rests, remains' *p.* reste
rustiġ adj. 'rusty'
rǣswa m. 'leader, director, king'

R*T
rǣt = rǣdeð 'reads'
rēot-að *pl.* 'they weep'
rīt = rīdeð 'rides'
rōt adj. 'cheerful'
rōtlīċe adv. 'happily'
rōtnes F. 'gladness'
rēotiġ adj. 'tearful'

R*TH
raþe adv. 'speedily' (hraðe)
rēðe adj. 'cruel, terrible'

rīð M. 'runlet'
ryðða m. 'mastiff'
rēðgodon *ppl.* 'raged'
rēðe-mōd adj. 'cruel, savage'
rēðen adj. 'wild'

R*W
rēow adj. 'rough. fierce' (=hrēoh)
rūiwes *gen.* of rūh 'rough'
rēwet N. 'rowing; a boat'
rōwan 'to row, propel'

S*
sǣ 'sea' *gen.* sǣ/sǣs
se M. 'the, that'
sē M. 'who, which'
sīe/sī/sȳ subj. 'be!; may be'
sīo F. 'the; which'

S*B
sibb F. 'concord, friendship'
ġesibb adj. 'related'
ġesibsum adj. 'peace-loving'

S*C
sacu F. 'struggle, conflict, dispute'; 'right to hold a court' *obl.* sæċċe
sac-eð 'struggles with, accuses'
sēc-ð 'seeks' *p.* sōhte
sēoc adj. 'sick, ill'
socc M. 'a sock'
sǣ-coccas *pl.* 'cockles'
secg M. 'people'; 'sword'; 'reed' *pl.* secgas
secgan 'to speak, say' *p.* sǣġde
sācerd M.. 'priest'

SC*
scō 'shoe' *pl.* scōn/ġescȳ
scua m. 'shadow, shade'
sceac-eð 'moves, departed' *p.* scēoc *pp.* scacen
scucca m. 'evil spirit'
ġescēad N. 'understanding, meaning'
ġescēad-eð 'divides; decides' *p.* ġescēd

scēad-eð 'scatters, spills'
sceadu F. 'shadow, shade' *pl.* sceadwe
ġescōd *p.* 'he injured, hurt' +*dat.*
ġescēadliċ adj. 'reasonable, sensible'
ġescēadlīċe adv. 'wisely, properly'
ġescēadwīs adj. 'prudent, clever'
sceadwe *pl.* 'shadows'
scūf-eð/scȳfð 'pushes, shoves' *p.* scēaf, scufon *pp.* ġescofen
sceaft M. 'shaft'
-sceaft suffix 'state of, condition'
ġesceaft FMN 'created being, creature; creation'
sceal 'must, has to; should, would' *pl.* sculon *p.* sceolde
sciell F. 'shell'
scōl F. 'school'
scolu F. 'troop, band'
scealc M. 'man; servant, member of a team'
sceolde *p.* 'had to, should' (sceal)
scield M. 'shield; protection'
scyld FM. 'offence, guilt, sin'
scyldiġ adj. 'guilty, sinful'
sculdra *pl.* 'shoulders'
scealfran *pl.* 'diving birds'
scilling M. 'shilling'
scima m. 'ray of light'
scam-að II 'it shames'
scamol M. 'stool'
scamliċ adj. 'shameful'
sciene adj. 'beautiful, radiant'
scīn-eð 'shines' *p.* scān
scīnende 'shining'
scinn(a) Nm. 'spectre, illusion; demon'
scinn-lāc N. 'sorcery'
scanca m. 'shin'
scenceð 'pours out (a drink)'
scand F. 'disgrace, scandal'
scendeð 'shames, blames'
scēap N. 'sheep' *pl.* scēap

ġesceap N. 'creature; creation, condition'
scip N. 'ship'
sciepp-eð 'creates, forms' *p.* scēop *pp.* ġesceapen
scōp/(ġe)scēop *p.* 'created'
scop M. 'poet, bard'
scipen N. 'animal shed'
scip-here M. 'naval force'
scyppend M. 'creator. i.e. God'
ġesceapennys F. 'formation'
scēar N. 'plough-share'
scīr F. 'authority, shire'; adj. 'gleaming, clear'
scier-eð 'cuts' *pp.* ġescoren
scūr M. 'shower, storm'
scearn N. dung
ġescærp *p.* 'cut'
scearp adj. 'sharp, shrewd, etc'
scierp-eð 'decks out'; 'sharpens' *pp.* ġescerped
sceorp N. 'garb, gear'
sceort adj. 'short'
scrid N. 'vehicle' *pl.* screodu
scrūd N. 'clothing, garb'
scrȳd-an I 'to clothe'
scrinc-eð 'shrinks, shrivels'
scrīð-eð 'moves, glides'
scræf N. 'cavern, den' *pl.* scrafu
scrīf-eð 'imposes, ordains; shrives' *p.* ġescrāf
scrīn N. 'chest, shrine'
tō-scēat *pp.* 'dispersed'
scēatas *pl.* 'areas, corner, region'
sceatt M. 'coin, money'
scēote f. 'trout
scēoteð/scȳt 'shoots: rushes' *p.* scēat, scuton
sceot, scyte N. 'a shooting'
Scottas *pl.* 'the Scots; Ireland'
scytta m. 'archer'
scēotend M. 'archer'
scēað 'scatters, spills' (= scēadeð)
sceðð-eð +*dat.* 'injures, hurts'
sceaða/scaða m. 'harmful or dangerous person; enemy'

[SC*]
sceaððiġ adj. 'dangerous'
scēawað 'gazes, scans' ppl.
   sceawedon
(fore)scēowað 'pre-ordains'

S*D
sǣd N. seed'
sǣde p. 'said, spoke'
sæd +gen. adj. 'full of. weary of'
sīd adj. 'wide, ample'
sīde adv. 'extensively'
sidu/siodu Npl. 'custom, habit'
   gen. sida
sydefull adj. 'virtuous'
soden pp. 'boiled, cooked'

S*F
sefa m. 'mind, heart'
seof-að II 'sighs'
seofon 'seven'
seofontiġ 'seventy'
sȳfre adj. 'chaste, abstemious'
sēfte/sōfte adj. 'soft, pleasing, comfy'
seofoða adj. 'seventh'

S*G
sǣg p. 'sank'
saga 'say!': subst. 'story'
sīġeð 'sinks, goes down'
siġe M. 'victory; setting, sinking'
siġe- 'victorious-'
sæġde p. 'said, spoke' pp. ġesæġd
seġl MN. 'sail'
seġlode p. 'sailed'
siġel 'the sun'
siglu Npl. 'necklaces. jewelry'
sæġl-rād M. 'sail-road, sea'
sǣgon/sēgon ppl. 'they saw' = sāwon
seġn MN. 'sign. banner'
senian II 'to make the sign of the cross'
sigor M. 'victory'

S*H
sēāh p. 'sank'
seah p. 'saw' (sēon)
seoh 'look!'
seht MF. 'agreement. settlement'
siehst, siehð 'you, he sees' (sēon)
sōhte p. 'sought'
ġesōhte p. 'sought out'
sīhð 'sinks' (sīgan)
ġesihð F. 'sight'

S*L
sāl MF. 'rope'
salu, salwiġ- 'dusky, grimy'
sāul F. 'soul'
sǣl MF. 'time. occasion'
ġesǣl-eð 'happens; binds, ties up'
sēl adj. 'excellent' cf. sēlra, sēlla
sele M. 'hall, house'
sel-eð 'gives, supplies' p. sealde
sēol- see seolh 'seal (animal)'
sol N. 'mud'
sūl/sulh N. 'a plough'
sȳl F. 'column, pillar'
selliċ = seldliċ 'rare, strange'
seolc M. 'silk'
onsǣled pp. 'untied'
ġesǣlde p. 'happened'
seld N. 'hall, palace; seat'
sealde p. 'gave' pp. ġeseald
seld-cūð adj. 'unusual, rare'
seldliċ adj. 'rare, strange'
seldan adj. 'seldom' comp. seldnor; superl. seldost
self/selfa pron. '(my)self, (your)self, (him)self, (them)selves, etc'
sealf F. 'ointment'
selfliċ adj. 'vain'
seolfor N. 'silver' gen. seolfres
seolfren adj. 'made of silver'
ġesǣliġ adj. 'happy, lucky'
seolh M. 'seal (animal)' pl. sēolas
sulh N. 'plough' gen. sylh/sūles

94

seolh-bæð	N. 'seal-bath, the sea'	symbel	N. 'feast, festival'
sealm	M. 'psalm'	samod	adv. 'together, simultaneously'
sol-mōnað	M. 'February'	sum-dæl	'somewhat'
sēlra	adj. 'better'	samn-að	'gathers' pp. ġesomnod
sēlost	adj. 'best, finest'	samnung	F. 'union, assembly'
sylst	'you give' (sellan)	samnunga/semninga	adv. 'straight away'
sealt	N. 'salt'	sæmra	adj. 'worse, inferior'
sylt-an	'to salt'	sǣ-maras pl.	'sea-horses, ships'
saltere	M. 'Psalter'	sēamere	M. 'seamster, tailor'
sealtere	M. 'salt-maker'	sumor	M. 'summer'
ġesǣlð	F. 'good fortune, happiness'	samtingesadv.	'at once'
ġesǣl-ð	'occurs, happens'	sām-wīs	adj. 'dull, not clever'
salwiġ	obl. of salu 'dusky'		

SL*

sleac	adj. 'slack, lax'
slecg	M. 'sledge-hammer'
slīd-eð	'slides'
slidor	adj. 'slippery'
sleġe	M. 'beating, slaughter'
slōg/slōh	p. 'struck, impelled' pp. ġesleġen
sleh-ð	'strikes'
slōh	= slōg
slēan	'to strike, beat, slay'
slǣp	M. 'sleep'
slǣp-eð	pl. slāpað 'sleeps' p. slǣpte
slīp-an	'to slip away' pp. slopen
slīt-an	'to slit; wound' p. slāt, slīton
slīðe	adj. 'ferocious, dangerous'
slāw	adj. 'slow, lazy'

SM*

smēagan/smēan	...hē smēað 'think, consider' p. smēade
smūgan	'to creep'
smēagung	F. 'thought, reflection'
smæl	adj. 'small'
smolt	adj. 'gentle, mild'
smylte	adv. 'mildly'
smaragdus	'emerald'
smirwan	'to annoint'
smēade	p. 'he thought'
smēðe	adj. 'smooth'
smið	M. 'craftsman, blacksmith'

S*M

sām-	'half-, partly-'
sam	conj. 'whether, or'
sam-	'in union, unison'
(swā) same	'the same, likewise'
sǣum	dat.pl. of sǣ 'sea'
ġesēm-an I	'to reconcile'
seom-að II	'tarries, continues'
sum	pron. 'a certain —, some' +gen. 'one of'
sim(b)le, symleadv.	'continually, ever'

S*N

sǣne	adj. 'slack, careless'
(ġe)sēon	'to see'
sīn	adj. 'his, hers, its'
sin-	(pref.) 'continual-'
sīen	'be' (subj. pl.)
sōna	adv. 'directly, at once'
sunne	f. 'Sun' gen. sunnan
sunu	M. 'son; descendant' gen. suna
ġesȳne	adj. 'visible, evident'
syn(n)	F. 'sin'
sanc	= sang 'sang'
senc-eð	'submerges, wets' p. sencte
sinc	N. 'treasure'
sinc-ġyfa	m. 'treasure-giver, lord'
sanct	M. 'saint'

[S*N]
sand N. 'sand'; F. 'sending, course of food'
send-eð/sent 'sends' *pp.* sended
send-on *ppl.* 'they sent'
sind/sindon 'are'
sund N. 'swimming; voyage; the sea'
ġesund adj. 'safe, healthy, whole' cf. ansund, ġesundful
sund-būende M*pl.* 'humans'
sundor adv. 'apart'
sundor- 'special, private'
(ā)sundrad *pp.* 'sundered (from)'
synderliċ adj. 'special'
syndriġ adj. 'separate, various'
sinniġ adj. 'criminal'
sang M. 'song, singing'; as verb, 'sang'
sing-eð 'sings' *p.* sang
syng-að 'he sins'
singal adj. 'perpetual, continuous'
Sunnan-ðāæġ M. 'Sunday'
sǣnra adj. 'slower, worse'
sin-scipe M. 'marriage, living together'
sun-stede M. 'equinox'
sent = sendeð 'sends'
sint 'are'
ġesynto F. 'health, welfare, prosperity'
sinoð F. 'synod'
sine-wealt adj. 'globular'

SN*
snīċ-eð 'sneaks along'
(be)snǣdan 'to cut, slash'
snofliġ adj. 'snotty'
snell adj. 'smart, prompt, bold'
snēome adv. 'speedily'
snyrġ-an 'to hurry'
snotor adj. 'clever, wise'
snyttru F. 'sagacity, wisdom'
snið-eð 'cuts' *p.* snāð, snidon
snāw M. 'snow'
snēow-an 'to hurry'
snīw-eð 'it snows'

S*P
sāp(e) 'sap, resin'
sūp-eð 'swallows, drinks'

SP*
spæċ 'spoke'
spēd F. 'success, resources'
spēd-eð 'succeeds, works well; is rich'
spell N. 'story, homily'
spell-ode *p.* 'spoke, narrated'
spill-an 'to spoil, destroy' *p.* spilde
(ā)spyl-ian 'to wash (oneself)'
spann-eð 'entices, persuades; joins, fastens'
spere N. 'spear. lance' *pl.* speoru
spyr-að 'pursues, tracks' *p.* spyrede
spar-að 'spares, saves'
spearc-ian II 'to spark'
spearca m. 'a spark'
spor N. 'trail, spoor'
spyrte f. 'basket, whicker trap'
sprǣċ F. 'speech, language'
spreċ-ð 'speaks' *p.* sprāċ, sprǣcon
spranc *p.* 'sprang, burst out, spread'
spring M. 'spring (of water)'
spring-eð 'springs up, arises' *p.* sprang
spearwa m. 'sparrow'
sprēot M. 'pike, spear'
sprytt-að *pl.* 'they sprout up'
spittan 'to spit; to dig in'
spīw-eð 'spit out, spew up'
spōw-eð 'it benefits, helps someone' *p.* spēow

S*R
sār N. 'pain, suffering'; adj. 'sore, painful'
sāre adv. 'sorely'
(for)sēar-að II 'withers'
searo N. 'cunning, art; trick, snare' *dat.pl.* searwum

searo-	'clever, artistic, ingenious'
syrċe	f. 'coat of mail'
serede	p. 'prepared, readied'
sāriġ	adj. 'sorry, unhappy'
sārg-ode	p. 'caused or felt pain'
sorg/sorh	F. 'sorrow, anxiety'
sorg-ian	to sorrow, care (for)' p. sorgode
sǣ-rima	m. 'coast'
searw-	see searo
searwum	adv. 'cunningly'
sierw-an	'to devise, entrap; to kit out'

S*S

sūsl	NF 'torment, torture'

S*T

sæt	'sat' pl. sǣton
sett-eð	'sets, places, ordains' pp. ġeset
ġeset	N. 'seat, dwelling'
ġesette	p. 'established, placed'
sit-eð/sitt	'sits, abides'
sot	adj. 'foolish'
setl	N. 'seat, throne, residence'
setlung	F. 'setting'
ġesetnes	F. 'ordinance: founding; arrangement, disposition'
Sæternesdæġ	M. 'Saturday'

ST*

stede	M. 'place, site'
stiċe	M. 'sting; stabbing pain'
stic-að	II 'stabs'; 'adheres' p. sticode
stōd, stōdon	'stood'
stede-fæst	adj. 'steady'
stæf	M. 'stave; letter' pl. stafas
stæf-ġefēġ	'syllable'
stefn	F. 'voice'
stefna	m. 'duty, turn; stem, tree-trunk, prow'
stīġ	FM 'path, track'
stīġ-eð	'ascends; descends' p. stāg, stigon pp. stiġen
stāh/stāg	'ascended, descended'
stīh-ð	'climbs' (stīgan)
stiht-eð	'directs, incites' p. stihte
stōl	M. 'chair, throne'
stalu	F. 'theft'
stela	m. 'stalk'
steall	M. 'stall; status'
ġestēaled	pp. 'extended'
onstealde	p. 'instituted'
-gestealla	m. '-companion'
stille	adj. 'still'
ġestill-an	'to stop, become still' pp. ġestilled
stȳle	N. 'steel'
styll-an	'to put into stalls; to rush, attack'
stealc	adj. 'steep'
ġesteald	N. 'residence'
stylnes	F. 'stillness'
stemm	F. 'stem, trunk' (= stefn)
stēam	M. 'moisture'
stān	M. 'stone'
ġestun	N. 'din; chaos'
stun-að	II 'crashes, roars'
stenc	M. 'odour, fragrance, smell'
stinc-eð	'smells, gives or receives smell; scatters
stand-eð/stent	'stands; remains, is' p. stōd
wið-stondan	'to withstand, oppose'
stund	F. 'short time; an hour'
stundum	adv. 'at intervals'
sting-eð	'stings, stabs' p. stang
stent	= standeð 'stands'
stunt	adj. 'stupid'
-stapa	m. '-walker'
stæpe	M. 'pace, step' pl. stapas
stæp-eð	'steps onward, goes' p. stōp
stēap	adj. 'lofty, projecting'
stapol	M. 'column, post'
stǣr	N. 'history'
star-að	II 'stares'
stēor	'steering, discipline'
stēora	m. 'steersman'
steorra	m. 'star, comet'
stīor-de	p. 'steered, directed'
stir	'confusion'

[ST*]
stȳr-eð   I 'steers, controls'
styr-ian   II 'to move, stir, incite'
           pp. ġestyred
styria   m. 'sturgeon'
stearc   adj. 'rigid, stern'
stēor-lēas adj. 'uncontrolled'
storm   M. 'storm; violent action'
styrm-eð   'storms, shouts'
stearn   M. 'tern'
steort   M. 'tail'
stēor-rōþer   N. 'rudder'

[STR]
strīċ-eð   'rubs; moves'
strēd-an   'to strew, scatter'
strūd-an   'to rob, plunder'
strugdon   ppl. 'scattered, spread'
           pp. strægd
ġestreht   pp. 'stretched'
strǣl   M. 'arrow'
strēam   M. 'current, water'
ġestrēon   N. 'profit, treasure'
strīn-eð   'acquires; begets' ppl.
           strȳndon
strȳnd   F. 'descent, stock'
strang   adj. 'strong, firm'
strengðu   F. 'strength'
strǣt   F. 'paved street'
stæð   MN. 'shore, bank' pl.
           staðas/staðu
stīð   adj. 'stiff, strong, strict'
staðol   M. 'foundation; station'
ġestaðol-ian   II 'to found,
           establish'
staðol-fæst   adj. 'fixed'
stōw   F. 'spot, site'

S*TH
sēað   M. 'pit, hole'
sēoð   'they see' (sēon)
sēoð-eð   'seethes, boils' p. sēað
sīð   M. 'occasion, journey,
           departure'
ġesīð   M. 'companion; warrior'
sūð   'south'
sīð-fæt   N. 'journey, expedition'
sōð   N. 'truth, certainty'; adj.
           'true, sure'

sōð-fæst   adj. 'honest, righteous'
sōðlīċe   adv. 'truly'
siððan   adv./conj. 'since, when'
sūðan   ady. 'from the south'
sūðerne   adj. 'southern'

S*W
sāw-eð   'sows (seed)' pp.
           ġesāwen
sēaw   M. 'juice'
sīow-(i)an   'to sew'
suw-að   II 'become silent'
sāwol   F. 'soul' gen. sāwle
ġesewenliċ   adj. 'visible'
sāwon   ppl. 'saw' (sēon)

SW*
swā   adv. 'so, just as'; conj.
           'as, like'
ġeswāc   p. 'ceased, failed'
swæċ   M. 'flavour'
swīċ-eð   'moves, goes; ceases.
           fails; betrays' p. swāc
swica   m. 'betrayer'
swiċdom   M. 'fraud'
swicol   adj. 'deceitful'
swef-eð   'sleeps; puts to sleep,
           kills' p. swæf, swǣfon
swefn   N. 'sleep; dream'
sweofot   N. 'slumber'
swift   adj. 'swift'
swēġ   M. 'sound'
sweġ-donppl. 'roared; made a
           noise'
swīġe   adj. 'silent'; subst.
           'silence'
swīg-að/swūg-að   'becomes
           silent'
swōg-an   'to roar, make a noise'
sweġl   N. 'sky, the heavens'
sweġle   adv./adj. 'brilliant,
           clearly'
swel-eð   'burns, smoulders'
swelċ/swilċ   pron. 'such a one,
           the same'
swylċe   adv./conj. 'likewise; as if'
swelg-eð   'swallows'
swealg/swealh pl. swulgon
           'swallowed'

swelt-an 'to die, perish' *ppl.*
swulton
swylt M. 'death'
swalewan*pl.* 'swallows (birds)'
sweoloð M. 'fire, heat'
swim-eð 'floats, swims' *p.* swom
swān M. 'swineherd; local youth'
swan M. 'swan'; —rād 'the sea'
swīn N. 'wild-boar, pig'
swenċ-eð 'harasses, troubles'
swinċ N. 'toil, hard work; hardship, problems'
swinċ-eð 'labours; struggles; is in trouble' *p.* swanc
sweng M. 'a stroke or blow'
sweng-eð 'rushes, flies'
swing-eð 'whips, flogs' *ppl.* swungon
swinsade *p.* 'sweetly sounded'
swinsung F. 'melody'
swāp-eð 'sweeps, rushes' *p.* swēop
swipu F. 'whip, scourge'
swēor MF. 'pillar'
swēora/swȳra m. 'neck'
swer-ian 'to swear
swearċ-eð 'becomes dark' *p.* swearc
sweord N. 'sword'
sworfen *pp.* 'ground up'
swirm-an 'to swarm (of bees)'
sweart adj. 'black, dark; evil'
swǣs adj. 'intimate, favourite'
swǣsendu N*pl.* 'dinner'
sweostor/swuster F. 'sister'
swāt M. 'sweat; blood'
swǣteð/swǣt 'sweats, exudes'
swēte adj. 'sweet, pleasant'
swutol adj. 'clear, evident'
sweotole adv. 'plainly'
swutel-að 'shows, displays' *p.* sweotolode
swǣð N. 'track, footprint' *pl.* swaðu
swaðul 'a flame'
swīþe adv. 'very'
swā-þēah adv. 'however'
swīðliċ adj. 'powerful'

sweðr-að II 'abates, subsides'
swīðor 'more strong(ly), quick(ly); of the right-hand'
swīðre 'on the right'
swīð-rað II 'is strong, prevails'

S*X
six 'six'
sēax M. 'hip-knife'
Seaxe M*pl.* 'the Saxons'
ġesyxt = ġesihð 'sees'

T*
tō prep. +*dat.* 'to, into, towards, at'
tō adv. 'towards, besides; too, also'
tō- 'to, towards; apart, asunder'
tēo 'I tug; I accuse'
tū 'two'

T*B
tō-blāweð 'blows away, scatters'
tō-breċeð 'breaks to pieces'
tō-brǣdeð 'broadcasts, disperses'

T*C
tǣċ-ð 'teaches; declares'
tūc-að 'ill-treats'
tō-cyme M. 'arrival, advent'
tācn N. 'symbol, sign' *pl.* tācn(u)
tācn-að II 'denotes, signifies' *p.* tācnode
tō-ēacen 'besides, in addition'
tō-cnāweð 'knows, recognises'
tō-ċorfeð 'cuts off, cuts away'

T*D
ġetēde *p.* 'prepared'
tīd F. 'hour; time; season'
tīd-eð 'happens'
tīode *p.* 'ordained'
tȳde *pl.* tȳdon 'instructed'
tō-dǣleð 'divides, distributes' *pp.* tōdǣlde

[T*D]
todæġ 'to-day'
tūdor N. 'offspring, descendant'
tȳdr-eð 'begets, produces'
tȳdre adj. 'weak, frail'
tō-drīfeð 'drives away, scatters'
tȳdreness F. 'frailty'

T*F
tō-flōweð 'flows away'
tōforan +*dat*. 'before' (time/place)
tefrung F. 'circle'

T*G
tīġ-eð 'ties'
tyġe M. 'tugging, leading'
tæġl M. 'tail'
ġetiġen *pp*. 'accused'
ġetogen *pp*. 'restrained'
tugon *ppl*. 'drew, tugged'
tōgædre adv. 'together'
tiġel(e) Ff. 'earthenware item'
tōġēanes adv. 'towards, against, in return'
tiger M. 'tiger' *pl*. tigras

T*H
tēah *p*. 'tugged'; 'accused'
ġetēah *p*. 'drew out'
tāh *p*. 'accused'
teohh-ian II 'to determine, assess, ordain'
tiohhung F. 'disposition, arrangement'
tō-hopa m. 'hope'
tȳhsð 'you draw, pull'
tǣhte, tēhte *p*. 'taught, demonstrated'
tīhteð/tīhð 'accuses'
tīhð 'draws, pulls'
tyht M. 'instruction'
tyht-eð I 'pulls; persuades; teaches'

T*L
tal-að 'counts, reckons'
tǣl F. 'blame, reproach'
ġetǣl-eð 'blames, reproaches'

ġetæl/ġetel N. 'number, count; tally' *pl*. ġetalu
tela/teola adv. 'well, correctly'
tel-eð 'estimates, tells, esteems' *p*. ġeteald
til-að II 'intends, strives'
till N. 'position, station'
til adj. 'good, excellent'
tōl N. 'tool'
toll MN. 'levy'
ġeteld N. 'tent'
telga m. 'branch'
telg M. 'dye'
tō-lȳseð 'loosens, dissolves'
tealt adj. 'unsteady, moving, tipping'
tilð F. 'farm-work; crop'

T*M
tam adj. 'tame'
tama m. 'tameness'
tēam M. 'lineage, offspring'; 'jurisdiction over guarantees'
tem-eð 'tames' *pp*. ġetemed
tīma m. 'time, period'
tīem-eð I 'begets, produces'
ġetimbru F. 'timbers, a building'
timbredon *ppl*. 'built'
tōmiddes +*dat*. 'in the middle of'
templ N. 'temple'
Temes(e) Ff. 'the Thames'

T*N
tān M. 'twig, shoot, stripe'
tēon to tug, pull; to accuse; to arrange, produce'
tēona m. 'pain, injury'
tēon- 'hurtful-'
tīen/tȳn 'ten'
tin N. 'tin'
tūn M. 'enclosure, garden; town'
tȳn-eð 'irritates, insults'
tuneċe f. 'tunic, coat'
be-tȳned *pp*. 'enclosed, shut'
ġetenge 'near to'
ġeteng-de *p*. 'closed with'
tunge f. 'tongue'

100

[T*N]
tungol   NM 'star, planet' *gen.*
         tungles
tintreġ N. 'torture'

T*P
tapor   M. 'candle'
tæppere M. 'tavern-keeper'

T*R
ter-eð   'rends, tears' *p.* tær, tæron
tēar   M. 'drop, tear'
(ā)tēorian, tēorað   'tire, cease' *pp.*
         ġetēorud
tīr   M. 'fame, glory'
tor(r)   M. 'tower; crag'
tor-að   'towers up'
tīr-ēadiġ(-fæst) adj. 'glorious, famous'
turf   F. 'turf, ground' obl. tyrf-
torfod   *pp.* 'stoned'
torht   adj. 'glorious, bright'
torn   N. 'anger; grief'
turn-að 'turns'
ymb-tyrnd *pp.* 'turned round'
turtur, turtla   Mm. 'turtle-dove'

TR*
trīo   = trēow 'tree(s)'
tred-eð/tritt 'treads (on)' *p.*
         treddode
ātrefed *pp.* 'drawn, depicted'
traht   M. 'text; commentary'
trum   adj. 'sound, fit'
untrum   adj. 'ill, invalid'
trym-að 'encourages, sets in order' *p.* trymede
trumliċ adj. 'firm, durable'
trumnes 'health, reliability'
trendel 'orb'
træpe   f. 'a trap'
tritt   'treads' (tredan)
trēow   N. 'tree(s); timber'
trēow   F. 'trust, faith, promise'
ġetrīewe adj. 'true, honest, loyal'
trūwað/trēoweð 'trusts'; *p.* trūwode

T*S
ġetǣse   N. 'usefulness'; adj. 'convenient, helpful'
tōsceot-eð   'shoots apart'
tōslit-eð   'tears apart' *p.* tō-slāt
tōsomne adv. 'together'

T*T
tōtwǣm-eð   'differentiates; breaks up'

T*TH
tīð   F. 'permission'; or verb (tēon) 'pulls; accuses; arranges'
tōð   M. 'tooth' *pl.* tēð
tīð-að   II 'grants'
tēoð   'they drag; they accuse'
tēoða   adj. 'tenth'

T*W
tāw-að   'readies; harries'
Tīw   'God of war; Mars'
tuwa   adv. 'twice'
tōweard adj. 'oncoming, approaching'; prep/adv. 'towards'
tō-weorpan   'to demolish' *p.* tōwearp
Tīwesdæġ   'Tuesday'

TW*
twā   'two'
twēode   *p.* 'was doubtful, uncertain'
ġetwǣfde *p.* 'divided'
twī-feald adj. 'double'
twiġ   N. 'twig'
twēġen   M. (twā F; tū N.) 'two' *gen.* twēġea *dat.* twǣm
twēoliċ adj. 'doubtful'
twelf   'twelve'
twǣm   *dat.* 'to two'
twǣm-an I 'to divide (into two)'
twēntiġ 'twenty'

T*X
tuxas   M*pl.* 'tusks'

TH*

þā	nom./acc.pl.	'the, those; who, which'
þā	adv. 'then'; conj. 'when'	
þe	acc./dat. 'thee'	
þe	(indecl.) 'which'	
þe	'the' (late texts only)	
þū	'you, thou'	
þē	'by which, in that'	

TH*C

ðaċ-ian	'to thatch'	
þæċ	N. 'thatch'	
þeċċan, þeċeð	'covers'	
þiċċe	adj. 'thick, dense'	
þicgan, þiġeð	'receives, consumes'	
þeċele	f. 'torch'	
þiċnys	F. 'thickness, opaqueness'	

TH*D

þēod	F. 'people, nation; country; language'	
ġeþēod-eð	'joins (with)'	
þēode	p. 'he flourished'	
ġeþēode	N. 'speech, language, nation'	
þēoden	M. 'leader, lord (of a tribe or nation)'	
þoden	M. 'whirlwind'	
þider	adv. 'on that side'	
þēodscipe	M. 'nation; community'	

TH*F

þaf-ian	'to permit, consent to; suffer, endure' p. ġepafode	
ġeþæf	+gen. 'consenting (to)'	
þēof	M. 'thief'	
ðȳflas	Mpl. 'bushes, undergrowth'	
ġeþafung	F. 'consent'	
ġeþofta	m. 'comrade, fellow crew-member'	

TH*G

þiġeð	'receives, consumes p þǣg, þǣgon pp. ġeþiġen'	

þugon	ppl. 'they flourished'	
þeġn	M. 'thane, official; attendant'	
þeġn-að	'serves' p. þeġnode	
þeġnung	F. 'service'	

TH*H

þēoh	N. 'thigh'	
þeahte	p. 'covered'	
ġeþeaht	N. 'divising'	
ġeþōhte	p. 'he thought' (þencan)	
ġeþōht	M. 'thinking, thought'	
þūhte	p. 'it seemed' (þyncan)	
þīhtiġ	adj. 'sturdy'	
ġeþeahtere	M. 'counsellor'	

TH*L

þol-að	'suffers, endures. survives' p. þolode	
ġeþyldiġ	adj. 'patient'	
þyling	F. 'planking'	
ġeþyld	F. 'patience'	

TH*M

þām, þǣm	dat.pl. 'to the, to those, to whom'	

TH*N

þēn/þeġn	'official, thane; attendant'	
þēon	'to prosper, do well'	
þen-eð	'stretches, extends'	
þīn	'your, thine'	
þone	acc.M.sg. 'the, that'	
þon	instr.MN.sg. '(by) the, that'	
þonne	adv. 'then'; conj. 'when; than'	
þun-að	'thunders, roars'	
þynne	adj. 'thin'	
þanc-að	'thanks'	
ġeþonc	'favourable thought, gratitude; thought, mind'	
þenċeð/þinċeð	'thinks (of)' p. þōhte	
þynċ-eð	'it seems' p. þūhte	
þancful, þoncol	adj. 'thoughtful, sensible'	
þindeð	'swells up'	

þing N. 'thing, matter, cause'
þing-ian 'to intercede; plan' *pp.*
    ġeþingod 'settled'
þengel M. 'prince, ruler'
ġeþungen *pp.* 'full-grown. well-grown'
þanon adv. 'from there, thence'
þīnen F. 'handmaiden'
þēnung F. 'service'
þunor M. 'thunder' *gen.* þunres

TH*R
þǣr adv. 'there'; conj. 'where'
þǣre *gen./dat.*F.*sg.* 'of/to the, that'
þāra *gen.pl.* 'of the, those'
þearf F. 'need, necessity'
þearfa m. 'poor man'
þearf 'needs (to), has to' *p.* þorfte
þurh prep. 'through. by means of'; adv. 'through, all over'
þǣr-rihte adv. 'directly, instantly'
þearl adj. 'strong, strict'
þearle adv. 'harshly, very'
þyrel N. 'hole'
þǣr-an 'therein, thereof'
þǣr-inne adv. 'therein'
þorn M. 'thorn (tree)'
ġeþuren *pp.* 'compressed'
þyrs M. 'giant'
þerscan 'to thresh'
þersc-wold M. 'threshold'
þyrst-eð 'thirsts'
þǣr-tō adv. 'thereto'

THR*
þrēa Fm. 'threat, attack'
þrī, þrēo 'three'
þri- 'three-, triple-'
ġeþrǣċ N. 'mob; violence'
þracu F. 'violence, onrush' *gen.* þrǣċe
þryġ-eð 'tramples on'
þrǣd M. 'thread'
þrēade *p.* 'afflicted'
þridda adj. 'third'

þrāg F. 'period of time, occasion'
þrǣġ-eð 'runs'
þrēaġ-eð 'threatens; punishes' *pp.* ġeþrēad
þroht M. 'heavy work, trouble'
þrǣl M. 'serf, slave'
þrim *dat.* 'to three'
þrymm M. 'power. glory; crowd'
þrēa-nȳd F. 'strict compulsion'
þring-eð 'presses on, crowds, cramps' *pp.* ġeþrungen
ġeþrang N. 'throng, crowd, tumult'
þrīnis F. 'the Trinity'
þrǣst-eð 'twists, torments' *pp.* ġeþrǣsted
þrīst adj. 'daring, adventurous'
þrostle f. 'thrush'
þrēat M. 'a crowd; coercion'
þrotu F. 'throat'
þrēatedon 'forced, rebuked, threatened' *pp.* ġeþrēatod
þrītiġ 'thirty'
þrȳð F. 'might, majesty'; adj. 'bold, mighty'
þrȳðliċ adj. 'valiant'
þrōw-ian 'to suffer' *p.* þrowode
þrōwung F. 'suffering, martyrdom'

TH*S
þās 'these'
þǣs *gen.*MN.*sg.* 'of the, that'
þǣs adv. 'after; to that (degree)'
þes 'this'
þēos 'this'
þus adv. 'thus'
þȳs *instr.*MN.*sg.* 'by this'
þǣs-liċ adj. 'suitable'
þūsend 'a thousand'
þēostru F. 'shadows, darkness'
þēostr-að II 'becomes dark'
þēostriġ adj. 'dark'

TH*T
þæt 'the, that'
þæt conj. '(so) that'

[TH*T]
þætte conj. 'so that'
þēotan, he þȳt 'roar, howl'

TH*TH
þȳð 'presses, pushes; forces'
þōþer M. 'ball'

TH*W
þāw-að 'thaws'
þēaw M. 'habit, custom, manners'
þēow MF. 'servant, slave'
þēow-eð I 'presses, forces' p. ðēwde
þēow-að II 'serves; enslaves'
þēaw-fæst adj. 'virtuous'
þȳw-an I 'to press, push'

THW*
þwyhð 'washes'
þwēal N. 'washing'
þwang M. 'a thong'
ġeþwǣre adj. 'harmonious, co-operative'
þweorh adj. 'bent; adverse' gen. þwēores
ġeþwǣrlic adj. 'congruous, in harmony'
ġeþwǣrlǣcð 'agrees; suits'
þwēorlic adj. 'contrary, awkward'
þwēor-tēme adj. 'perverse, contrary'

TH*X
þūx-að 'darkens'

W*
wā, wēa M. 'woe, misery'; wā! 'alas!'
wē 'we'
wō = wōh adj. 'crooked, perverse'

W*B
web N. 'weaving, tapestry'

W*C
wāc adj. 'weak, feeble'
wāc-eð 'becomes weak'
wac-ian, wac-eð II 'awakes, is born'
weċ-eð 'rouses, wakes s.one up'
wīċ N. 'village; trading-post'
wīc-að 'dwells'
wiċċa m. 'wizard'
wucu F. 'week' gen.pl. wucena
wecg M. 'lump (of metal)'
wecg-að 'they disturb, move about'
wicg N. 'horse'
wāc-liċ adj. 'pathetic'
wacol adj. 'wakeful, alert'
wǣċn-eð 'comes into being'
wæċċende, waċiende 'watchful'
wīċing M. 'Viking'

W*D
wād N. 'woad'
wadu Npl. 'waters, sea'
wǣd F. 'dress, clothing; sail'
wæd-eð 'moves' pl. wadað p. wōd(on) pp. ġewaden
wēd-eð I 'rages, goes berserk' ppl. wēddon
wedd N. 'pledge, agreement'
wēod N. 'herb; weed'
wōd adj. 'mad'
ġewōd p. 'went; pervaded'
wīde adv. 'widely'
wudu FM 'wood, timber; tree; a wood' gen. wuda, wudes
wǣdl F. 'poverty'
wǣdla m. 'a poor person'
Wōdenesdæġ 'Wednesday'
weder N. 'weather; storm'
wīdor adj. 'wider'

W*F
wāf-að 'is amazed; admires'
(be)wǣfed pp. 'enwrapped'
wēofod N. 'altar'
wīf N. 'woman'
wīf-cȳð 'female company'
wǣfels MN. 'a cloak'
wīf-mann M. 'woman'
wāfung F. 'display, spectacle'

104

wæfre adj. 'wavering, errant'
wæfersīn F. 'spectacle, display'

W*G
wāg M. 'wall'
wag-edon *ppl.* 'wagged, swayed'
wǣġe N. 'cup'
wǣġ 'wave; the sea'
wǣġ- 'wavy-patterned-'
wǣġ-eð 'troubles, upsets' *pp.* ġewēġed
weġ M. 'way, path, route' *pl.* wegas
weġ-eð 'carries, supports'
wīġ N. 'conflict, battle'
wīġ- 'war-'
wiga m. 'fighter'
wiġ-bed M. 'altar'
wigl-ian 'to make magic'
wiglung F. 'sorcery'
wæġn M. 'waggon, vehicle'
wīġend M. 'warrior'

W*H
wāh = wāg 'wall'
wōh adj. 'bent, kinked, bad'
wī-haga m. 'war-hedge, shield-wall'
wōh-hǣmed N. 'adultery'
wiht, wuht FN 'being, creature'; adv. 'at all'

W*L
wālā!, wālāwā! 'alas!, woe!'
wæl N. 'slaughter, violent death' *pl.* walu
wǣłē 'on deep water'
wel adv. 'well, easily'
wel- 'almost, nearly'; 'well, good'
Wēalas M*pl.* 'the Welsh'
weall M. 'wall, rampart'
weall-eð 'seethes, rages, boils' *p.* weoll *pp.* ġeweallen
wile 'he wishes'
wil- 'willing, friendly'
willa m. 'will, desire'; sim. ġewill
wiell(a) Mm 'spring, fountain'
wōl 'plague'

wull F. 'wool'
wealc-an 'to roll' *p.* weolc *pp.* ġewealcen
weolc M. 'whelk'
wolcn N. 'cloud; sky'
wǣl-cyriġe f. 'witch'
weald M. 'forest'
ġeweald N. 'power, authority'
wilde adj. 'wild'
weald-eð 'rules, controls' +*gen.*
wolde *p.* 'he wished, would'
ġeweald-leðer N. 'rein'
wealdend M. 'ruler, esp. God'
wuldor N. 'glory'
wildēor N. *pl* 'wild beasts'
weliġ adj. 'rich, wealthy'
welig-að 'prospers'
wæl-hrēow adj. 'savage, bloodthirsty'
wealh-stod M. 'translator'
wel-hwā 'anyone'
wel-hwǣr 'nearly everywhere'
wealh M. 'foreigner, slave, Welshman' *gen.* weales
wylm/wielm M. 'surge'
w(e)allende 'raging, boiling'
wiln-að 'wishes, longs (for)' *p.* wilnode
wilnung F. 'desire, longing'
weleras M*pl.* 'lips'
wǣl-stōw F. 'battlefield'
welt/wilt 'he rules' +*gen.*
wilt 'you wish'
wielt 'rules, governs'
wealw-að 'rolls; shrivels up'

WL*
wlanc adj. 'splendid, proud'
wlǣtta m. 'loathing'
wlīt-an 'to look upon' *p.* wlāt
wlite M. 'beauty'
wlitiġ adj. 'beautiful'
wlǣtta m. 'loathing, nausea'
wlite-sēon F. 'spectacle'

W*M
wamm M. 'stain; corruption'
wem-eð 'defiles, smears'
wōma m. 'noise, alarm'

wamb   F. 'belly'

W*N

wēn   = wæġn 'cart'
wana   m. 'lack'
wan-að   'lessens, declines' pp.
    ġewaned
wēn   FM. 'hope, expectation';
    also wēna m.
wēn-eð   'hopes, imagines,
    expects' p. wēnde
wen-að   'accustoms, trains' p.
    ġewenede
wīn   N. 'wine'
wine   M. 'friend'
win-eð   'struggles, competes'
ġewinn-an   'to beat, win' pp.
    ġewunnen
ġewinn   N. 'toil, hardship;
    conflict'
won/wan adj. 'colourless,
    lustreless,dark; feeble'
ġewuna   m. 'custom'
wun-að   'dwells, inhabits;
    remains' p. wunode
wyn   F. 'joy'
wand   p. 'twisted, curled,
    meandered'
bewand   p. 'clasped'
wend-eð 'goes, wends; changes'
āwend-eð 'turns, alters, translates'
wind   M. 'wind'
wind-eð   'curls, twists; flies, leaps'
    p. wand
wund   F. 'wound'
wunode   p. 'dwelled'
wunden   adj. 'wound up, twisted'
āwunden pp. 'woven, twisted'
wundon   ppl. 'wound' (wendan)
wanung   F. 'diminution, waning'
wīn-ġeard   M. 'vineyard;
    ?vine'
Wendel-sæ   'the Mediterranean'
wyn-lēas adj. 'joyless'
wandr-að 'wanders, flies about'
wundor   N. 'a marvel'
wundr-að 'marvels at' p. wundrode
wundrum adv. 'marvellously'
wang/wong   M. 'a plain'

wange   n. 'jaw, cheek'
wan-hāl   adj. 'unwell'
wynnum adv. 'joyfully'; or *dat pl.*
    of wyn
ġewuneliċ   adj. 'customary,
    usual'
wynsum   adj. 'pleasant, charming'
winstre   f. 'heft-hand'; adj. 'left'
went   'goes' (wendan)
winter   N. 'winter; years'
winde-winċle   f. '(peri)winkle'

W*P

wǣpn   N. 'weapon'
wēp-eð   'weeps' p. wēop
wōp   M. 'crying, lamentation'
wǣpned   adj. 'armed; male'

W*R

wār   N. 'seaweed'
war-að   'is wary; guards'
-ware, -waran   pl. 'inhabitants,
    citizens (of)'
wǣr   F. 'good faith; treaty'
wær   adj. 'wary, cautious'
wer   M. 'man'
wet   M. 'weir; trap for fish'
wer-að   'guards, defends' p.
    werode
wærc   N. 'pain, suffering'
weorc   N. 'work, labour,
    suffering, pain'
ġeweorc   N. 'work, built structure'
wyrċð   'works, makes, does'
weard   M. 'keeper, guardian'
werod   N. 'crowd; an army
    subdivision'
word   N. 'word, speech, saying'
wurd-on ppl. 'became, were' pp.
    ġeworden
wyrd   F. 'event, outcome; fate,
    history'
for-wyrd F. 'damnation'
wyrd-an   'to spoil, damage, injure'
    pp. werded/āwyrded
wariġan   'to beware'; 'to guard,
    inhabit'
wēriġ   adj. 'weary, exhausted'

wearg	adj. 'accursed, wicked'; subst. 'outlaw, criminal' pl. wergas	wreċeð/wriċð	'drives, expels, utters' p. wræċ, wræcon pp. ġewreċen
wierġed	adj. 'accursed'	wrīdende	'growing, thriving'
word-hord	'word-resource, vocabulary'	ġewrēġedpp.	'agitated'
worhte	p. 'made, did' pp. ġeworht	wrig-að	'advances, twists'
		wrugon	'covered' pp. ġewriġen
ġewyrht	FN 'work, deed; desert'	wrāh	p. 'covered'
wyrhta	m. 'maker, creator'	wrīh-ð	'he covers' pp. wriġen
wærliċ	= wær adj. 'wary'	wrōht	F. 'accusation, dispute'
woruld	F. 'world; the contemporary world, life'; tō worulde 'for ever'	wrohton	ppl. 'wrought, made'
		wrēon	'to cover'
		wrenċ	M. 'trick'
		wræst	adj. 'capable, excellent'
woruld-	'worldly, secular-'	ġewrit	N. 'writing; a writ, a book'
wær-loga	m. 'liar, traitor'		
wearm	adj. 'warm'	wrīt-eð	'he writes' p. wrāt
wyrm	M. 'reptile; dragon'	wrætliċ	adj. 'ornamental, unusual'
wyrm-cynn	N. 'reptile, serpent'	wrītere	M. 'writer, scribe'
warn-að	II 'warns'	wreð-að	'supports, upholds' pp. wreþyd
-waran	= -ware 'citizens'		
wæron	'were'	wrīð-eð	'twists, wraps, binds'
weorn-að	II 'fades'	wrāð	adj. 'angry': subst. 'foe'
worn/wearn	'large number, crowd; many'	wraðe	adv. 'angrily'
		wraðu	F. 'support'
wyrn-eð	'denies, forbids'	ġewrixl	N. '(ex)change, alternation'
weorp-eð/wyrpð	'throws, casts' pp. worpen		
		wrixl-eð	'exchanges'
weras	M.pl 'men'		
wyrs	'worse'; wyrst 'worst'	**W* S**	
wyrt	F. 'herb, plant'	wæs	p. 'was'
wyrtrum(a)	Mm. 'root'	wēas	'by chance'
wyrtwal-að	II 'uproots'	wīs	adj. 'wise'
waroð/wearoð	N. 'shore, beach'	wīsa	m. 'leader'
wearp	p. 'became'	wīse	f. 'way, fashion, manner'
weorð	adj. 'valuable'; subst. 'value, worth'	wīs-að	'directs, guides' p. wīsode
		wis-að	'demonstrates' p. wisode pp. ġewissod
weorð-að	'honours, worships' p. wurðode		
		ġewiss	adj. 'certain, dependable'
wyrð/weorðeð	'becomes. is (+pp.)'	wōs	N. juice' -
for-weorðeð	'perishes'	wasc-eð	'washes'
weorð-mynd	'honour, distinction'	wīsdom	M. 'wisdom'
		ġewissliċē	adv. 'certainly'
WR*		wesan	'to be'
wracu	F. 'revenge, punishment' gen. wræċe	wissung	F. 'instruction, guidance'
		wāst	'you know'
wræċċa	m. 'exile, outcast'	wēst-eð	'lays waste'
		wist	F. 'food; existence'
		wiste	p. 'he knew

107

[W*S]
west   adv. 'west(wards)'
wistlung F. 'whistling'
wæstm   M. 'growth'; *pl.* wæstmas
          'crops, fruits; condition'
wēsten   'wasteland, wilderness'
westan   'from the west'
wēstende 'devastating'
westerne 'westerly'
West-Seaxe   *pl.* 'the West Saxons'

W*T
wāt   'he knows' *pl.* witon
wǣt   adj. 'wet'
wǣta   m. 'moisture'
wǣt-eð   'wets' *p.* wǣtte
wīte   N. 'punishment, penalty'
wīt-eð   'blames, punishes'
wīt-eð   'departs' *p.* ġewāt *pp.* ġewiten
wit   'we two'
wit-an   'to know'

Heart of Albion

Publishing folklore, mythology and local history since 1989

Details of all Heart of Albion titles online at **www.hoap.co.uk**